Contents

Also by Dr. Paul Baker and Dr. Meredith White-McMahon

The Hopeful Brain: NeuroRelational Repair for Disconnected Children and Youth

Better Behavior - Positively!

Brain-Based Strategies and Solutions

Dr. Meredith White-McMahon
Dr. Paul W. Baker

About This Book

This book is for anyone living with or working with young people. It can be a challenging job and some days it is downright difficult! No two days are ever the same and it can certainly keep you on your toes. But when everything is running smoothly, it can be fulfilling, rewarding, and even exciting. Using the latest in neuroscience and relational theory, this book will help guide you to understand why young people behave the way they do and provide suggestions to help you deal more positively and effectively in transforming this challenging behavior.

This book provides a variety of ways to implement positive behavioral support. It should be used actively, not just read through. Along with exercises, we have provided opportunities to answer posed questions and to record your thoughts. The goal is to challenge your thinking and your perceptions. All the exercises are suitable for use by individuals, teams, or groups.

Throughout the book you will see three icons indicating three different types of exercises:

Self-Reflection Sheets: There are 16 throughout the book. Each one will ask you to engage in reflective thinking about a concept you have just encountered in the book and how it might apply to you and the young people with whom you work.

Strategy Sheets: Here you will find an abundance of supportive suggestions for dealing with different types of challenging behavior. As we will say more than once in the book itself, there is no "one-size-fits-all" approach for encouraging better behavior.

Activity Sheets: These sheets either provide case-oriented scenarios or real-life structured situations to allow you to plan and practice.

Chapter 1 introduces you to our Neurorelational Framework, a strengths-based approach that we believe can set the stage for better behavior. You will also find a list of our basic assumptions about behavior.

In Chapter 2, the need for social connections and relationships will be explored. You will find out why relationships really do matter and how to create sustainable relationships through the suggested strategies.

The four core NeuroRelational attributes—safe, significant, respected, and related—are introduced in Chapter 3. How the brain can influence behavior is discussed in more detail.

Chapter 4 focuses on the impact of chaos, stress, and trauma. It presents suggestions of ways that you can successfully work towards better self-regulation with these young people.

The neuroscience behind the NeuroRelational Framework presented in this book is found in Chapter 5. This chapter gives you concrete strategies for helping young people whose brains and body development are not in sync.

Conflict management versus crisis support is discussed in Chapter 6. The focus of this chapter is momentary management: what do you do, right there, in the moment, to stop conflict from becoming a crisis situation. We explore ways that you can intervene using brain-based support strategies to meet a young person's unmet developmental needs.

In each of these chapters, you will find: story examples (of course, the names and some situational details have been changed); self-reflection questions to consider; activities to reinforce the concepts; and strategy sheets to add "tools to your behavior toolbox."

Chapter 1

The NeuroRelational Solution
for Challenging Behavior

....

I am a part of all that I have met. Lord Tennyson

Hope for Challenging Behavior

Are you struggling with a young person's challenging behavior? Well, there is hope! Today's professionals are faced with ever increasing demands to meet a greater diversity of needs of young people. Within this book, evidence will be presented that demonstrates the importance of what modern brain research, combined with years of relational practice, is now showing. All behavior is needs driven. Troubled young people express their needs in a variety of ways. They can "act out" in a physical or aggressive manner or they can "act in" by withdrawing. These challenging behaviors often occur when the young people we work with do not have the skills to meet those needs or the ability to communicate to us that they need help meeting those needs. Everyone needs to feel safe, significant, respected, and they need to relate to and with at least one other person.

Behaviors can, and will, change when trained adults are therapeutically connected with challenging young people, allowing them to better understand their needs. A multitude of scientific disciplines is now proving that, when provided with appropriate knowledge and targeted strategies, adults become extremely powerful agents of transformation, even in the most serious of cases. This is very encouraging news! Research also tells us that without such training we will spend a great deal of time trying to figure out what to do to stop challenging behavior.

Behavioral Change Is Not Complex

Behavioral change does not need to be complex. In fact, the primary goal of this book is to help simplify the behavioral change process, making it less threatening and more approachable by everyone, no matter the educational background or years of experience of the professional. To begin this process, it is important to introduce an innovative approach known as the NeuroRelational Framework. The

NeuroRelational Framework is a powerful, positive, strengths-based approach designed to promote core principles and practices that help caring adults connect with young people to promote behavioral transformation. It is believed that when this transformation happens, the lives of troubled young people are changed for the better. Trained, caring professionals are the pivotal part of this process!

Understanding how the various systems within the brain function provides professionals with the basic knowledge to increase the effectiveness and strength of relationships and of behavioral support. This knowledge can be used to transform challenging behavior into more functional and successful outcomes. In addition to knowledge, we become relationally empowered to understand how to interact with others more efficiently and effectively. Over time, these interactions will form therapeutic relationships. These relationships encourage natural strengths to surface within young people, helping them to overcome adversity. They involve transactions that continually impact experience and development throughout their lives. This, in turn, will lead to increased motivation, more resilient personal skills, and, finally, successful behavioral outcomes!

Pulling It All Together

Transformation is an integrative process. Part of simplifying the transformative process is in understanding the unique history of each young person. It focuses on the various biological, regulatory, relational, ecological, cultural, and academic needs that may be lacking or missing from their history. Empowered with this knowledge, therapeutic adults and challenging young people will partner together to understand how new people and ecologies in their life can assist with "reimbursing " them with needed skills and experiences to become resilient.

Young people formulate beliefs and behaviors based on their prior experiences. From their perspective, they might feel, from previous interactions, that people called "teacher" or "youth worker" or "foster parent" have always meant a "negative experience" for them. So if your role is one of these, the assumption is that any interaction they have with you must automatically be negative. While their view of you may seem unusual, particularly if you see yourself as a caring individual, "the way that we make meaning very much influences, and perhaps even determines, how we respond" (Garfat, 2002) to different people and situations. Everybody "makes meaning" based on their previous experiences combined with the "here and now" because all learning is based on prior bits of learning. The goal of the NeuroRelational approach is to stretch or push challenging young people beyond the boundaries within which they normally think and feel. This change, or transformation, provides a new mindset allowing 'our' young people (that is, those with whom we in the field work daily) to take different actions than they may have taken in the past, leading to empowerment, growth, and strength.

NeuroRelational Beliefs

No matter what the history of the young person might encompass, there is a fund of what we term NeuroRelational strategies that people can use with challenging young people. This model is underpinned by the following beliefs:

Belief #1   We are a result of our experiences, both good and bad. The brain is responsive to every experience.

Belief #2   People, not theories, are primary in relational change.

Belief #3   The brain can, and will, change for the better when trained individuals understand its basic functions and needs.

Belief #4   Relationships and ecological/environmental factors create states and traits in young people.

Belief #5   NeuroRelational knowledge is key to transformation and resilience.

Belief #6   NeuroDynamic Interventions are powerful approaches that provide positive, relational, and brain-based support to troubled young people.

Why Do We Behave the Way We Do?

Behavior is an individual's observable response to their environment (the things and people around them). From the moment we are born, every experience we have shapes how we learn to respond. If our experiences are healthy and our developmental needs are met, our behavior is generally appropriate for the cultures in which we exist. Over the course of our lives, we watch and model the behavior that we experience. When our experiences with those close to us are less than ideal and our normal developmental needs are not met consistently or not at all, we experience higher levels of stress and anxiety. In these situations, it is common for defensive, difficult behavioral patterns to become a part of our everyday repertoire. Our behavior can be an attempt to deal with those feelings. Our brains are continuously developing as we experience life and these experiences will shape and alter the pathways in our brain. "Experiences shape not only what information enters the mind, but the way in which the mind develops to process that information" (Siegel, 1999, p. 16).

Behavior and Relationships

There are three assumptions that underpin the strategies you will read about in this book. These assumptions are interconnected and equally important. Our young peoples' experiences to date may have shaped their brains and influence how they see life and consequently how they behave. It is the transformative experiences they will have, with people like you that can change their lives for the better.

The behaviors that our young people exhibit and your connection with them are intertwined. Behavior is a way of trying to tell us something, something that may not be readily apparent to us. In fact, we may think a behavior is driven by something else entirely. Understanding behavior is vital to becoming an agent of change, but we can't fully understand any behavior unless trust exists between the adult and the young person. Without that, they will not be willing to open up and share information that helps us to see the behavior for what it is. This can be graphically represented in the following way:

The Interconnection of Behavior and Relationships

Why Relationships Matter

Our brains develop through our interactions with others. Connecting and having experiences with other people is vital to survival. The connections or relationships that we have with others are what shape our brains and become our natural environments (Cozolino, 2006). We are social beings who are wired to seek out close connections with others. This need to connect and belong is a basic psychological need (Baumeister & Leary, 1995). It is part of what makes us human.

Safe

Positive relationships allow us to feel **safe** so that we can explore and learn. When we feel safe and supported, we don't have to spend all our time and energy on survival tasks like reacting to danger or finding food. We are able to explore our world, engage with others to combine our skills and talents, and successfully create something greater than the sum of its parts. Positive relationships allow us to feel like we matter.

Significant

Positive relationships make us feel **significant**. Feeling significant makes us feel good and this in turn allows us to lead healthier, longer lives (Hawkley et al., 2006). Being positively connected to others reduces aggression and increases pro-social behaviors (Pavey, Greitemeyer, & Sparks, 2011).

Respected

Positive connections to others help us understand who we are and feel a part of something larger than ourselves. Once we are connected and are an accepted part of a group, we need to feel **respected** to be able to effectively interact and take risks within that group. Respect is fundamentally tied to our existence as social beings that live and survive in groups (Nadler, Malloy, & Fisher, 2008). When the people we are connected with ignore us, threaten us, or make us feel judged or rejected, that feeling of respect is lost and we will strive to make other connections to replace it.

Related

When we are connected with others who make us feel safe, significant, and respected, we can experience things with them, understand their perspective, and work together for a common goal. In other words, we can **relate** to them and they to us. Once we can relate to others, we are then able "to walk a mile in their shoes" and learn to be compassionate and empathetic.

People Change People – Not Theories

The important thing to keep in mind is that **people** are the key to this transformation. Theories don't change people; people change people. In order to provide positive growth experiences for your troubled young people, you need to understand the way brain systems work because the way you work with the brain and the body is extremely important in the development of relationships. You will be able to choose the right strategies and play an important role in their transformation. Knowing that our brain's neural pathways can change throughout life based on interactions with others and new and different experiences, is very good news. It provides hope. We need hope if we want to be motivated to work for change. When we are hopeful, we look for strengths instead of weaknesses or deficits and build on them. Think about something you are hopeful about. You will likely do whatever you can to make it happen because it matters to you. If you are not hopeful, you are not very likely to invest much time or energy into it, are you?

We need to look at the young people we work with through a hopeful lens. Perhaps we need to re-examine not only the way we think about our young people but also the way we work with them, changing our focus from a perspective of deficit to a perspective of strength. It is our job to help our young people find hope. Without hope there will be no change. Think of this as your new job description: it is your job to help the young people you work with find and restore hope in their lives. And here is some more good news. Hope is a two-way street. If you can help your young people find hope through the relationships that you make with them, you will also experience a positive change—your experiences with your young people will shift from confrontation to connection. Doesn't that sound motivating?

Self-Reflection 1

Think about a young person that you work with now, or in the past, that has made your days less than fulfilling. Divide a piece of paper in two. Label one side "Deficits" and the other side "Strengths." Come up with a list of characteristics that the young person exhibits that are considered deficits. Use as many lines as you need. Then, thinking about the same young person, come up with a list of characteristics they exhibit that are considered strengths. You may have to be a little creative initially but keep going until you can come up with as many strengths as deficits. Remember that strengths are in the eye of the beholder. For example, "street smarts" is a strength if you are homeless.

Deficits	Strengths

Look at both lists. Which one best describes the young person? Does the list of strengths help you to see the young person in a different light? Do you find it easier to see them in a positive or a negative light? Why?

How did you do? Was one column easier to complete than the other? Did you find that after some consideration, really both lists described that young person? We are not asking you to deny problems or challenges, we are simply asking you to challenge your perception and focus so that you have something with which you can make a connection and build a relationship. Change is all about the relationship. Focusing on strengths is a good start. Our troubled young people need relationships that are caring and stable where they can connect, develop a sense of trust, and be able to talk about the issues, frustrations, and good things in their lives.

How We Develop and its Impact on Behavior

All human beings progress through stages as they develop. Their bodies mature, their cognitive abilities, emotional regulation, and appropriate and healthy social skills develop and improve. Development is fairly sequential and predictable. One stage builds on the acquisition of skills in the previous stage. However, there is a great diversity in the rate and specifics of development in adolescence. Age and/ or physical appearance are not necessarily valid indicators of development.

Developmental psychologist Erik Erikson (1993) proposed eight developmental stages that begin when we are born and continue through to old age. Erikson believed that each stage was characterized by the competition of two different forces creating a "crisis" that must be resolved to obtain the appropriate "virtue" for that stage. According to Erikson, these conflicts focus on either developing or failing to develop a psychological quality. During these times, the potential for personal growth is great, but so is the potential for failure. According to Erikson's theory, the resolution of each crisis and the attainment of each virtue is dependent not only on the individual's own traits and abilities but also on the support of family, peers, and society. Failure to complete a stage successfully can result in a reduced ability to complete further stages and therefore a more unhealthy personality and sense of self. These stages, however, can be resolved successfully at a later time. Erikson also notes that there is overlap in the transition between the stages and that the stages should not be thought of as levels of achievement or permanent as psychosocial development is not clear cut and/or irreversible.

The major forces adolescents face are "identity versus role confusion," with the goal of obtaining and maintaining a personal identity and belief system that allows them to be a productive and contributing member of society. Erikson put a great deal of emphasis on the adolescent stage, feeling it was a crucial time for developing a person's identity. When the balance between the opposing dimensions of the "crisis" occurs, the conflict of that stage is resolved and the individual is ready to move to the next stage, early adulthood (Erikson, 1993).

Erikson's (1993) Stages of Development

Age	Conflict	Resolution/Virtue
Infancy (0-1 yr)	Trust vs. Mistrust	Hope
Early Childhood (1-3 yrs)	Autonomy vs. Shame	Will
Play Age (3-6 years)	Initiative vs. Guilt	Purpose
School Age (6-12 years)	Industry vs. Inferiority	Competence
Adolescence (12-19 years)	Identity vs. Confusion	Fidelity
Early Adulthood (20-25 years)	Intimacy vs. Isolation	Love
Adulthood (26-64 years)	Generativity vs. Stagnation	Care
Old Age (65-death)	Integrity vs. Despair	Wisdom

Is Behavior Developmentally Appropriate?

There are certain behaviors that are typical for an age and stage but are inappropriate in most situations; there are behaviors that are atypical and very inappropriate. How we deal with each of these is very different. Erikson's theory of psychosocial development is one explanation of what is considered to be a "normal" developmental process. What happens if development is abnormal, as in the case of children who grow up in ecologies of neglect, abuse, and/or trauma? Trauma can have an enormous impact on the development and behavior of young people. Dr. Mary Wood (2007) believes that the current social, emotional, and behavioral status of any young person needs to be taken into consideration so that behavior management strategies are appropriate for their developmental stage, not just their chronological age. If development is delayed due to particular life experiences, young people may be displaying cognitive or socio-emotional behavior that is not typical or appropriate for their chronological age. And we all know uncharacteristic age-inappropriate behavior is never well received either by the adults or the peers of that young person. In fact, if inappropriate behaviors continue to persist over time, the problems of that young person will compound dramatically.

Basic Assumptions about Behavior

While you will read about these assumptions in greater detail in the chapters that follow, here are a few things to think about before you read further:

Behavior Meets Needs: If a young person continues to engage in a particular behavior, it is meeting their needs—even if they are continually getting into trouble for it. This is very powerful. The behavior may seem counterintuitive to you, but it doesn't to them. In fact, it may be very functional.

Never Assume: The assumptions you make about the causes or reasons for behavior will directly impact how you choose to deal with it. If you think it is a personal attack or the young person is doing it on purpose, you will respond in a counter-aggressive manner. If you assume they are "old enough to know better," you will likely resort to punishment of some kind instead of focusing on teaching adaptive replacement behaviors.

Personal Viewpoint: Your own personal experiences and even your training will influence your assumptions about why young people behave the way they do. This is normal. These assumptions may be conscious or unconscious, but they are there. Maintaining an open mind is critical to seeing things differently and to creating change.

Work Hard or Work Smart: We spend a great deal of time trying to get young people to stop doing the things we don't like rather than on teaching them new and better skills and replacement behaviors. We need to change our focus first. This isn't easy because it is very tough to see beyond the challenging behavior.

Brain Development: Our brains are dependent on and develop through interactions with others. We can reduce conflict and develop more positive ways of connecting to these troubled young people. We believe the key to this connection is found in the power of both our brains and relationships—what we call a "NeuroRelational" approach.

Stress, Trauma, and Chaos Make It Tougher: Chronic stress, chaos in the home and/or environment, repeated negative experiences, and/or traumatic events will affect brain development profoundly, and consequently will affect behavior.

One Size Does Not Fit All: One size does **not** fit all when it comes to behavior support. Everyone's experiences are different as are their individual needs. Everyone needs to feel safe, significant, respected, and related. When we are able to connect with young people and help them meet their needs appropriately, there will be better behavior.

Self-Reflection 2

Do you agree with the following statements? Circle your choice and briefly explain your reasons.

1) All behavior, even challenging behavior, serves needs. (Agree/Disagree)

_____

_____

_____

2) Our responses to behavior do not need to be positive to reinforce it. (Agree/Disagree)

_____

_____

_____

3) Every behavior that violates a program rule should have a consequence. (Agree/Disagree)

_____

_____

_____

4) Making instructional and/or environmental accommodations for young people with behavior problems is not fair to others around them. (Agree/Disagree)

_____

_____

_____

5) Punishment teaches new behaviors. (Agree/Disagree)

_____

_____

_____

6) The quality of the relationship of the young person and adult impacts student behavior. (Agree/Disagree)

_____

_____

_____

Chapter 2

Social Connections and Relationships

· ·

Coming together is a beginning; keeping together is progress; working together is success. Henry Ford

The Importance of Relationships

Relationships matter! The impact that we have on young people is enormous. Most people who make the career choice of working in the helping fields have a deep-rooted passion for the job and for young people. We enter the field and truly want to make an impact. When things get tough and frustrating, our efficient brains attempt to solve the challenges of the moment. Realistically, there is no simple solution because a one-size approach to behavioral support does not fit. However, we believe there is a way to reduce conflict and develop more positive ways of connecting to troubled young people. We believe the key to this connection is found in the power of both our brains and relationships—our NeuroRelational approach. It is now known that our brains are dependent on and develop through interactions with others. Throughout our lifetime, we need positive people and supportive ecologies for optimal survival, growth, and well-being. By tapping into the power of relationships and the brain's ability to adapt and change, this powerful strengths-based approach provides a way to address even the most challenging behavior and obtain positive outcomes. And it all begins with a change in perception.

Behavior, the individual's observable response to their environment, or what we see another person "do," operates in a constantly changing social and emotional ecology. Young people need to feel safe, significant, respected, and related in order to grow and develop well. Focusing on these needs is important as they help us to understand what drives behavior, motivates people to strive and achieve, and provides the hope needed that will form the basis for change.

We Are Our Experiences

In *The Hopeful Brain: NeuroRelational Repair for Disconnected Children and Youth*, we explain that we are the result of our experiences, both good and bad, and that the brain is responsive to every experience. "From our first breath to our last, everything and everyone in our environment affect how we grow and develop" (Baker & White-McMahon, p. 3). Psychologists define perception as "the organization, identification, and interpretation of sensory information in order to represent and understand the environment" (Pettinelli, 2015, p. 21). Our experiences in life create our perceptions of the world and the people around us. We learn how to function within our ecology by studying the behavior of others around us by using parts of the brain called mirror neurons.

Learning from Others

We are constantly watching and studying those around us. Mirror neurons, found in the orbito-prefrontal cortex behind the eyes, are specifically in charge of imitating others. Within our brain, we are constantly mimicking the behavioral presentations of others in an effort to learn more about the people with whom we interact. This constant evaluation allows us to read a variety of people and their intentions. We build an internal resource "manual" that we consistently call on without even knowing. This internal "manual" enables us to predict the intentions of others by comparing their actions with the actions of others in our past.

Over time, our experiences help us create a template (our perceptions) that guides the way we think about or understand someone or something. Our perceptions are affected by our motivational and emotional states and unusual situations. Depending on the situation and the motivational or emotional state, we can react to or perceive something in different ways. In a difficult or unfamiliar situation, particularly where we are stressed, we can often "see what we want to see." When we have a lot of similar experiences in a particular situation, we learn to make finer perceptual distinctions and we learn new kinds of categorization. This predisposition to see things in a particular way then drives our behavior. These behaviors are used to successfully navigate the world around us and are reinforced, or not, by our experiences that occur when we behave the way we do. It is important to note that while everyone develops perceptions and behaviors in the same way, the *experiences* that we have can be very different. Different experiences lead to different perceptions, which in turn lead to different behaviors.

It is often helpful for you to reflect on a challenging young person that you work with. When you are with that young person, your two worlds "collide." You bring to the table all your life experiences, all the past and present people and environments you have encountered that have shaped your brain and perception. You even bring your expectations of your future experiences. The young person brings their experiences and expectations. If they are similar, you both behave in a similar manner, but if they are not, perceptions and responses will be anything but similar. In fact, the young person's behavior will probably be so different from yours that it makes little or no sense to you and you will question why they continue to behave in this manner. The problem with this way of thinking is that it is biased by your perceptions and experiences. The behavior you are seeing doesn't work for you on any level because it doesn't match your perceptions (or your experiences). But—and this is a big but—it does work for them. I absolutely guarantee you that it does! And probably the less you can see that, the more effective it is for them. We assume that if the outcomes of behavior don't match what we think they should be, it is ineffective or just plain wrong and should be extinguished. Their mirror neurons have taught that young person the effectiveness of this behavior through their experiences. If the behavior was not effective in helping them navigate their environment, they would stop it and do something else.

Organizational Beliefs and Practice... Why Congruency Is Important

Behavior cannot be changed in isolation; nor can a single caring person change it. It will require everyone involved in an organization or associated with the young person, taking a vital role in a behavior's transformation. Identifying processes that continually assess and provide for therapeutic support are essential. Let's explore some basic considerations.

All organizations operate using two very important leadership tools: vision and values. The intertwining of these aspects becomes critical for the success of any organization.

Vision

Theoretically, the vision describes what the organization wants to achieve or what they want to look like at some point in the future if they are growing or transforming. The vision provides direction and a clear focus for employees. It also addresses the appropriate behaviors that are needed for success. The vision provides a tool for measuring progress, and a common vision can be a tool for reducing conflict between different functions within an organization.

Values Matter

Values describe how we will behave within the organization and with our clients or stakeholders (in our case, the young people and the significant people in their lives). Values define what the organization thinks is important in its life and when done correctly, organizational values help us to understand ourselves and our client's needs better, provide a code of conduct, and form a basis for trust. Combined, these are the key things that organizations believe. "Believing" is great and is not usually the problem. Where organizations often struggle is in the implementation of the vision and values, or the "doing." This is not deliberate, for the most part. The leaders believe in the vision but find that they just can't get their employees engaged and actively participating in that vision. The end result is everyone "doing their own thing."

In the caring or helping professions, we are faced with a multitude of complex tasks and issues, so often the vision and values for these professions is a theoretical approach that helps the staff "make sense of things, maintain the capacity to think, and find meaning in the most difficult situations" (Barton, Gonzalez, & Tomlinson, 2012, p. 30). Working from a theoretical base provides consistency and reliability in the work we do with young people. It also provides a research and evidence base that we know has worked for others, giving us a sense of hope.

Caring professions must deal with the changing needs associated with working with people and that requires a certain amount of flexibility. Cookie-cutter approaches will definitely not work well because we are all inherently different. But without a theoretical base and understandable practice that is common to all staff, we run the risk of doing more harm to both the young person and the adults working with them by not encouraging or allowing learning, growing, and changing (Bloom, 2005; 2013). You know a helping organization is "doing" their "believing" when you see a common language being used and a thoughtful staff that makes an effort to not let assumptions or labels drive their thinking and responding. They see young people through a hopeful lens full of opportunity instead of a negative lens of bad behavior and problems. In essence, caring professions should encourage critical thought and sensitivity within the parameters of the theoretical base rather than a one-size-fits-all prescriptive approach. Organizations need to focus on what Dr. James Anglin, a professor at the School of Child and Youth Care at the University of Victoria in Canada refers to as "working in the best interests of the children" (2013).

Working in the Best Interests of the Young People – James Anglin

In his article, 'Working in the children's best interests: differences that make a difference' (2013), Anglin reiterates the need for a framework of understanding to lead to organizational consistency, reciprocity, and coherence. Think of organizational consistency as everyone working as a team with a mutually agreed-on set of values and principles instead of each staff member working from an individual philosophy and "doing their own thing." This does not mean that there cannot be individual style and approach differences but that, overall, a consistent philosophy drives all interactions. This includes supervisors, management, and outside agencies. Reciprocity in this context refers to mutual and equal give and take in communication and relationships. There are few surprises—everyone gets and gives what they expect. Finally, Anglin (2003) used the term coherence to refer to the degree to which all of the behaviors of everyone in the organization flow and work well as a whole. Anglin reminds us that this is a struggle as most helping organizations are far from young people's ideal life situation. However, we need to aim continually to be the best we can be for them.

Anglin believes it can be an existing well-developed model or one internally developed, but in either case it must have appropriate principles and approaches that keep the "best interests" test at the center of any decision-making. Because the principles and values of these types of models tend to be rather broad, he suggests that the following staff behaviors must be present to ensure that organizations are actually "walking their talk:"

1. **Listen and respond with respect**: Everyone wants to be valued as a person. Respectful interaction helps develop a sense of self-worth and dignity.
2. **Communicate a framework for understanding with young people**: Doing so helps them understand their needs and wants better and to learn to self-advocate appropriately.
3. **Build rapport and relationships**: Connection and relationships lead to a sense of relatedness and belonging.
4. **Establish structure, routine, and expectations**: We all need these things. They give us predictability, a sense or order, and a "mental and emotional safety net." This is where trust begins to grow.
5. **Inspire commitment in young people**: This gives them a sense of pride in what they do, develops a sense of values, and encourages loyalty.
6. **Offer emotional and developmental support**: This helps them develop a sense of caring and experience mastery.
7. **Challenge thinking and action**: Just like we asked you to self-reflect earlier, challenging thinking and action allow for learning, growth, and success.
8. **Share power and decision-making**: Marginalized young people often believe they have no choice. Modeling this behavior gives them back a sense of personal power and the ability to learn to make good decisions.
9. **Respect personal space and time**: We learn best when we make mistakes, learn at our own speed, and still feel respected.
10. **Discover and uncover potential**: You can do anything you put your mind to and work hard enough for. When you feel capable, you have hope.
11. **Provide resources**: This can range from young people helping each other to management providing appropriate funding. It helps develop a sense of gratitude and generosity.

When Behavior is Based in Pain

Anglin (2003) coined the term "pain-based behavior" during his four-year study of residential care. He believes that responding to this pain is the biggest challenge faced by those working with troubled young people. Most of the young people we work with have had a great deal of experience with pain. It is long standing and deep seated and is often "glossed over" by those around them. Since we know that we can only respond to others based on our experiences and perceptions, Anglin felt that the term "pain-based behavior" was important because it reminds us that the challenging behavior we often have to deal with comes from these experiences. It is not personal and we do not want to respond to pain by creating more pain. That is never in the best interests of a young person.

Self-Reflection 3

Review the 11 staff behaviors that Anglin believes must be present if we have the best interests of a young person in mind.

1) Which behaviors do you feel that you incorporate into your daily work with young people?

_____

_____

_____

_____

_____

2) Which behaviors do you not incorporate or could incorporate more effectively?
What do you need to do this?

_____

_____

_____

_____

_____

3) We all bring our past history into the mix when faced with challenging behavior. Remember that the young person's mirror neurons are reading your reaction as you approach. What do you think they generally see (positive or negative)?

_____

_____

_____

_____

_____

4) Do you have expectations or beliefs that impact how you respond to challenging behavior?

_____

_____

_____

_____

_____

Pain, Punishment, and Discipline

What makes humans different from all other species is the fact that we have a thoughtful, decision-making, problem-solving part of our brain located right behind our foreheads called the pre-frontal cortex. It can sift through our stored life experiences (memories) and help us make the best decisions possible based on what we know from our experiences so far. Like all other animal species, we also have a reactive, non-thinking part of our brain, which we need for survival in life-and-death situations. This part of the brain is primitive and purely reactive. The brain systems involved with punishment and pain reside in this primitive part of the brain so they, too, are purely reactive and non-thinking. When we resort to punishment, it reduces the human experience to a primitive level. Relating to a challenging young person on this kind of primitive level will only breed a mirrored, primitive response from the young person. It will ensure that a cycle of non-thinking, reactive behavior is perpetuated between the young person and the adult. Wise adults utilize the brain's ability to think, and they decide to guide young people to logical choices that will serve them well in the moment and later in life.

Self-Reflection 4

Think back to when you were much younger. What kinds of discipline or punishment did you experience (home/daycare or sitter/school, etc.)?

Consider the following four questions.

1) What type of discipline or punishment was used?

_____

_____

_____

_____

2) How did it make you feel?

_____

_____

_____

_____

3) Was it effective? Why do you think it was or wasn't effective?

_____

_____

_____

_____

4) If you had been the adult in that situation, what, if anything, would you have done differently?

_____

_____

_____

_____

Discipline Promotes Growth

Punishing young people is quite different from disciplining them. The Latin root for discipline is "discipulus," which comes from the verb "discere," meaning "to learn." Discipline uses positive ways of guiding young people to develop self-control and confidence. Positive discipline relies on the adult engaging the problem-solving part of the brain and making decisions based on helping young people better understand their own behavior and respect themselves and others.

Effective discipline has everything to do with the adult controlling his or her counter-aggressive feelings in the moment and making decisions that help a young person develop self-control and personal accountability in the long term.

A growing awareness that punishment only breeds primitive, non-thinking reactions has prompted many of us working with young people to explore more restorative practices, ones that create environments that make young people feel safe, significant, respected, and related to those around them.

Restorative Practices

Restorative practices promote relationship building and problem-solving. Instead of punishment, young people are encouraged to reflect on and take responsibility for their actions, come up with plans to repair damage, and work on more appropriate ways to respond (Riestenberg, 2002). The fundamental premise of restorative practices is that people are happier, more cooperative and productive, and more likely to make positive changes when those in positions of authority do things *with* them, rather than *to* them or *for* them (The International Institute for Restorative Practices, 2009). These practices focus on community, capacity, and respectful relationships.

Creating Sustainable Relationships

We believe there are four attributes that all human beings have and that all behavior is an attempt to meet those needs. Everyone needs to feel **safe**, **significant**, **respected**, and **related**. Dysregulated or dysfunctional behavior occurs when these needs are not being met. As we are social beings and need others to survive and survive well, we need people and relationships to meet our needs. These needs are so strong that when the normal attempts we make to meet our needs don't work, we find another way to do it because the needs remain even when relationships fail. Unhealthy artificial attachments or strategies like gang affiliation, substance abuse, aggression, and self-injury become substitutes for the positive healthy ones. To avoid this, we all need to be connected to other people who are positive influences. One connection is good but more are better, particularly for our troubled young people.

Connection starts with micro-interactions. These are seemingly small things that can build into big experiences. A smile and a "hello" as you pass in the common area or hall, the use of a name, a hand on the shoulder are all examples of micro-interactions. Sometimes just being there is enough. Being present sets the stage for new positive experiences that help repair old painful ones. Micro-interactions can yield macro results! But they are just the start. There are several other factors, anchored in developmental psychology, that must be present to create a sustainable relationship in child and youth-care professions: *trust, attunement, empathy and compassion*, and an *ecological sense of community*.

Trust

Trust is the foundation for connecting positively with young people. All humans are social beings and their brains are prewired to connect with one very significant person: their mother or primary caregiver. This attachment was the first interactive relationship, and it depended on nonverbal communication. The quality of the attachment that people experienced will determine how they will relate to other people throughout their life. It established the basis for all verbal and nonverbal communication in future relationships. If the attachment experience was confusing, frightening, or absent, they internalized those relational patterns, which shaped the brain. Those early experiences became wired in the brain and later came to function as unconscious templates shaping the success or failure of future close relationships, emotional and self-regulation, the ability to rebound from disappointment, and the ability to trust.

Developmental psychologist Nicholas Hobbs believes that "trust between child and adult is essential… the glue that holds teaching and learning together" (1994, p. 245). He notes that if people have had relatively normal attachment experiences, they grow up with the expectation that most adults care about them and are there to help. They believe adults can be trusted until they prove otherwise. However, troubled young people that we work with have generally not had optimal early attachment experiences so they see adults, including us, as untrustworthy. Have you ever met someone and had the feeling that something about him or her was just not "right"? You can't put your finger on it but you just have this bad feeling? Daniel Goleman calls this our "radar for insincerity" (Goleman, 2006, p. 22). It is our survival brain, the reactive non-thinking part providing an "early warning system" to keep us safe. Our young people's early warning system goes off a lot in this regard and it is because of their experiences. It doesn't matter how good your intentions, how much you like kids, or how caring you really are, their brains are wired to survive and their life experiences are telling them you are dangerous because you are an adult. Without trust and understanding, no growth or change can occur. The only way you can get to growth is to provide alternative experiences for young people that allow them to interact with a trustworthy adult. Talking about trust does very little, but experiencing trust—being able to get close to someone without being hurt physically and emotionally—will allow a young person's brains to rewire and change. It is important to realize that building trust is not an easy process. It is an incremental process (Maier, 1987) and it takes a great deal of time and repetition.

So how do we get there? The key is being there with the individual and letting them realize that first basic need: that they can be safe with us. While that sounds relatively straightforward, you will likely find that it is anything but. Troubled young people's experiences often tell them that adults are not worthy of their trust. Adults have not been there for them in the past. They have punished or even rejected them when they didn't behave in a manner the adults deemed appropriate. They have been hurt, physically and emotionally, by people who "looked and sounded" just like you. In an attempt to protect themselves, they test you. Are you just another adult who will talk a good game but not follow through when the going gets tough? And they will make it tough—over and over again. We call these "trust trials."

Trust trials are actually a good thing because they provide us with the opportunity to prove to our young people that we are different and worthy of their trust. Think of it as a two-way dance between a young person and adult and the adult and the young person. It can go both ways. Regardless of their intensity and no matter how much they test our resolve, when we stay committed to young people we provide a safe place for them to be themselves. Through positive and accepting verbal and nonverbal behavior, we provide new and better experiences. With a nurturing, trusting relationship, a significant adult can play a big role in the brain's ability to change (Cozolino, 2006; Schore, 1994). When our troubled young people feel safe and secure in the relationship, they are then able to explore and consider different strategies and behaviors.

Self-Reflection 5

Consider the following behaviors. For each one, write down one reason for the behavior that comes to mind immediately. Then think about other reasons for the behavior that you are seeing. The reasons can be both physical and emotional.

1) You are reprimanding a young person and they yawn and put their head on their arms.

Reason:

_____

_____

_____

Alternative Reason:

_____

_____

_____

2) You are praising a young person after they have shown behavioral growth and they turn away, ignoring you. You persist and they tell you angrily to shut up, that it is no big deal.

Reason:

_____

_____

_____

Alternative Reason:

_____

_____

_____

Can you think of any other reasons for these types of behavioral responses? If you asked a friend or co-worker, could they come up with other possible reasons?

Are we always right when we make assumptions about the reasons why young people behave the way they do?

What does this tell us about assumptions that we often make about our young people?

Attunement

Attunement describes how a person reacts to another's emotional needs and moods. If people are well attuned to others, regardless of their emotional state, their language and behaviors will be appropriate. Attunement is the way people focus on the internal world of another. It is how "… another person harnesses neural circuitry that enables people to 'feel felt' by each other. This state is crucial if people in relationships are to feel vibrant and alive, understood, and at peace" (Siegel, 2007, p. xiii).

Attunement is being aware of, and responsive to, another person; much of attunement is nonverbal. Our survival brain reads nonverbal communications, checking to see if they match what is being said and done as a way to determine if we are safe. It looks at eye contact, tone of voice, facial expressions, and overall body language. If the brain detects that nonverbal messages we are sending do not sync with what is being said, it will override the words.

Being attuned with young people involves the following:

1. **Giving your full attention**: This is not the time for multi-tasking. Stop whatever else you are doing and give them your undivided attention (Pryce, 2012).
2. **Real listening**: Take the time to figure out what they really mean and what they really need, not just reacting to the words or actions. Ask questions to better understand where they are coming from not just the immediate presenting issue. Be sensitive to changes in emotions (Jones, 2011).
3. **Understanding**: Work to understand their point of view and not only being concerned with getting your point across (Morrow & Styles, 1995).
4. **Be sincere and genuine**: They can spot a phony a mile away! Pay particular attention to your nonverbal behavior (Morrow & Styles, 1995).

Attention to behavior and accurate interpretation of it are important. Being attuned will help. When you notice a young person's situation and feel their feelings, it will not only increase your understanding of individual needs but it can improve the relationship as well. Win–win!

Empathy and Compassion

Once we are attuned, we can then move forward by being able to relate to our young people. The most powerful way to relate to others is through empathy—the ability to interpret and truly understand how another person feels. This can lead to compassion—acting on that understanding of how they feel (McDonald & Messinger, 2014). These words are often used interchangeably, which can lead to some confusion, so for the sake of this discussion we will differentiate between the two this way: *empathy* is a way of thinking while *compassion* is an action.

In addition to being able to understand how others feel and see things from the other person's perspective, one should also be able to regulate one's own emotional response (Decety, 2010). You may be thinking that these abilities seem like normal adult social skills but even adults can have trouble with these. For instance, some people might refrain from helping others who are in need, not because they lack empathy, but because they may not know how to cope with their own emotional reactions to the other person's situation.

We have often heard staff members make comments like "That kid has no conscience. He/she doesn't care about how others feel." We are all born with the capacity to be empathetic but we need to learn it through appropriate role modeling. If a young person has not had that kind of behavior modeled, they do not have the necessary experiences to learn how to be empathetic (LeSure-Lester, 2000).

So what do we do if they don't have these experiences? We give them new experiences that teach them how to be empathetic and compassionate, as well as helping them learn to deal with their own emotions. Keep in mind that many young people with turbulent histories have dysregulated brain systems that are not yet equipped to manage the world around them. So we need to help them raise their levels of competence by modeling and providing "in the moment support" or proactive practice sessions. When young people see that adults are competent and capable, their brains allow them to connect more deeply and the relationship is fortified and ripe for more intensive growth. This won't happen overnight. It takes 50 to 200 practice events for the brain change we are looking for to occur, but the good news is—it *will* happen.

Ecological Sense of Community

Nothing happens in isolation. Everything in a young person's ecology affects how they grow, develop, and change. In the 1960s, psychologist Urie Bronfenbrenner developed an ecological systems theory to explain that a young person's growth and development are affected by everything in themselves and in their environment. He considered all the different aspects of the environment (the young person's ecology) that influenced his development, including: the immediate relationships or organizations with which the young person interacts (microsystem); how the different parts of a young person's microsystem work together for the sake of the young person (mesosystem); and the other people and the other influential people and places with which a young person interacts indirectly, such as parents' workplaces, extended family members, or the community (exosystem). The more encouraging and nurturing these relationships and places were, the better the young person's growth and overall well-being. In addition, Brofenbrenner also took into consideration the macrosystem, which was the largest and least direct part of the young person's ecology but which still had a great influence over a young person. The macrosystem included things such as the government, cultural values, and the economy (Bronfenbrenner, 1979).

Bronfenbrenner believes that, as a society, we have allowed economic expectations and pressures to create instability and unpredictability in family life as we work longer hours in a desire to "have it all" (Addison, 1992). Young people do not have the consistent interaction with significant adults that is necessary for optimal development. According to his theory, if the relationships in the immediate microsystem break down, the young person will not have the skills and abilities to explore other parts of their ecology. Young people looking for the attachments and connections that should be present but aren't now look for attention in inappropriate places. Young people who have had poor relational experiences in their microsystem also tend to see their future as unfulfilling and not worth working for. They need that connection with a significant adult to have hope.

Young people express their needs in a variety of ways. They can act out, being physical and aggressive and "in your face." They can also act in, where they withdraw and "check out." Many times the act-ins are not noticed, sometimes until it is too late. Whether they act-in or act-out, their needs are just as great. We need to attend to both and create a new ecological sense of community where we can be the significant adults who can help both groups meet their needs.

Strategy Sheet 1: Building Positive Relationships

A. **Micro-interactions result in macro-relationships**. Brief positive interactions improve self-regulation and build up the emotional bank account. Think of the emotional bank account as a metaphor for the strength of the relationship. You can make "deposits" and strengthen it, or you can make "withdrawals" and weaken it. It is normal for both to occur over time, but if you want the relationship to flourish you need to make more deposits than withdrawals. With young people, it helps to have a credit balance in the account for those times when things go wrong and you have to impose consequences.

B. **Be respectful** (even when it is tough). Respect is a two-way street. It is important because it is an appreciation, admiration, and recognition of a person being worth something. When we are respected, we feel significant and related. Young people model the behavior that they see. If you treat them in a courteous, thoughtful, attentive, and civil manner, they will be more likely to treat you the same way.

C. **Be clear and consistent**. Clarity and consistency are the main ways we learn how to predict things. When something is clear and consistent, we can rehearse it and incorporate it until it becomes a part of us. When we can predict accurately, we have a sense of security. Vagueness and inconsistency, on the other hand, create anxiety. Young people who have clear, consistent rules with predictable consequences are less likely to "push the limits" and constantly test you by misbehaving. They quickly learn that "no" means "no." If you are not consistent, "no" means argue, fuss, and carry-on until you give in. You get annoyed and time gets wasted. Being consistent is hard; not being consistent is harder.

D. **Have high but reasonable expectations**. Expectations tend to be a self-fulfilling prophecy. Young people will behave in the way you expect because your expectations send a subtle and sometimes not so subtle message about their intelligence, value, and capability. Expectations are not just something you talk about; they are something you model in your interactions with them, making them apparent they are what you really believe.

E. **Communicate with letters & journals**. Letters and journaling can help young people release the stress of their daily lives as well as provide them with insights into their problems and the world going on around them. It can help them make sense of the changes in their lives or can be a way of releasing the events of the day without acting out. Journaling can also focus on the positive by opening up possibilities in their lives and helping them to think through things and make better decisions.

F. **Involve other adult mentors**. A Canadian five-year study that followed the experiences of almost 1,000 young people registered with Big Brothers Big Sisters agencies found that those with a mentor were significantly more confident academically and considerably less likely to display behavioral problems (Centre for Addiction and Mental Health, 2013). The supportive relationships that can develop from mentoring help young people go through challenging life transitions and help in dealing with stressful changes at home or within their programs.

G. **If at first you don't succeed, keep trying!**

Reimbursements – How to Meet Those Unmet Needs

Many challenging young people miss critical experiences in their lives that are vital to optimal development, and these missing elements are often further impacted by broken relationships. Having few-to-no meaningful or safe connections with significant adults, they may seek out artificial attachments through street gangs, sexual promiscuity, or substance abuse. They may also develop pseudo-relationships through, or with technology, drugs, or alcohol. Feelings of abandonment, hurt, and anger may lead young people to lash out or withdraw from their environments. These makeshift attachments provide artificial connections that are often transitory and short lived, not fulfilling the needs of the brain's social instincts. However, when we meet these needs appropriately, either through repairing, reshaping, or replacing the broken or missing elements in the life of a young person, we are providing "reimbursement." We have found six general areas that are most often in need of reimbursement.

Relational: experiences with people that have been damaging, inconsistent or absent.

Experiential: missing life experiences that are typical of those in the same developmental age range critical to normal skill acquisition.

Biological: basic body and health needs.

Regulatory: self-control and appropriate expression of emotions across a variety of ecologies.

Academic: filling essential educational gaps that are critical for success in life.

Eco-Cultural: prior unique experiences, beliefs, values, and language that affect present day interactions with other people.

Our troubled young people need trustworthy, attuned, empathetic adults like you in their lives who are willing to provide these kinds of reimbursements and start the transformation process. These young people can and will change if the right adults are involved in their lives.

Self-Reflection 6

Think about a challenging young person that you work with.

1) What challenging behaviors do they exhibit that concern you?

_____

_____

_____

_____

2) What experiences have they had (or not had) that might lead to these behaviors?

_____

_____

_____

_____

3) Based on your answers to #2, what reimbursement(s) do you think they may need?

_____

_____

_____

_____

How Our Biases Impact Our Responses

We all have biases—the tendency to believe that some people or ideas are better than others. These biases often result in unfair treatment of people around us. Our biases are conscious (explicit) and unconscious (implicit). We are aware of our explicit biases and use words or actions to convey them. We are not, however, aware of our implicit biases. Our implicit biases are activated automatically and include our emotions and feelings about people and ideas (Bobula, 2011).

David Amodio, an associate professor of Psychology and Neuroscience at New York University, has spent the last decade studying implicit bias using electroencephalograms (EEGs) and functional magnetic resonance imaging (fMRI) to track brain functions related to bias. He found that part of implicit bias comes from fear conditioning, a process that allows a neutral stimulus to make us fearful because we have learned to associate it with something negative. Amodio believes that this fear conditioning makes our implicit biases easy to learn and almost impossible to unlearn. However, Amodio's research also suggests that the brain can control unwanted biases if we are aware of them (Amodio & Devine, 2008).

The anterior cingulate cortex, a part of the brain involved in cognition can detect the activation of implicit biases. It can also detect conflicts between how we want to think and the automatic behaviors that conflict with it. For example, we may want to believe that we treat all people equally, but our behavior shows that we actually do not. The anterior cingulate can send a message to the dorsolateral frontal cortex, the part of the brain that regulates our abilities to evaluate, inhibit, and act on social and emotional information, allowing us to consciously override these implicit biases (Amodio, Devine & Harmon-Jones, 2008).

When you enter your workplace, are you subject to these perception biases with your young people? Of course you are—we all are. But are you aware of them? Maybe you are, but unless you have really thought about it, you likely are not. So we are going to ask you to think about it now.

Think about those challenging young people again. We all form opinions of people and things both consciously and subconsciously—our judgment is rarely free of biases. Before judging the proverbial book by its cover, be sure to collect all the relevant facts. What are your perception biases?

We react to behaviors based on our own cultural experiences. The things we were taught to respect as acceptable behavior contribute to our biases. We assume that people who behave like we do are the same as us and are therefore good, while people who do not behave as we do are different and may not be good.

Our young people also come to us with biased perceptions. We can be perceived as being just like all others who have held a similar role to us. They will see you as being the same as every other teacher, youth-care worker, foster parent, or justice worker that they have had experiences with in the past. Perception is a two-way street.

Self-Reflection 7

Consider the following behaviors: using street language or incorrect grammar; burping publicly after eating; arriving late for a class, meeting, or appointment; shaking hands when you meet someone.

1) How do you react to or interpret these behaviors?

_____

_____

_____

_____

2) What other possible meanings could these behaviors have?

_____

_____

_____

_____

Chapter 3

The Four Core NeuroRelational Attributes

· ·

It is easier to build strong children than to repair broken men. Frederick Douglass

Four Core NeuroRelational Attributes

In order to survive and survive well, we all have four critical areas of need that must be met. We all need to feel *safe, significant, respected,* and *related.* These are fundamental needs that everyone has in common, and all behavior is simply an attempt to meet those four needs. While we are all programmed to work towards meeting these needs, the ways in which they can be met are virtually unlimited. Understanding these needs, and the different ways people attempt to meet them will help us to work more effectively with our young people.

Safe

Why is feeling safe important? When we feel safe, we can regulate stress-related emotions and develop new, healthier relationships with those around us. When we feel safe, we are more likely to be relaxed, open to new experiences, and able to benefit from them. As Ratey (2001) explains, new experiences are the best way to create new and better pathways in the brain.

In the 1940s, Abraham Maslow, a pioneer of humanistic psychology (a holistic approach to human existence) focused on what motivated, directed, and sustained human behavior. He developed what has become known as a hierarchy of needs: *physiological, safety, love and belonging, esteem,* and *self-actualization.*

Self-actualization
self-fulfillment and seeking personal growth

Esteem
achievement, mastery, independence, status,
self-respect, and respect from others

Social
friendship, affection and love from family,
friends, and/or co-workers

Safety
shelter, security, order, law, stability,
freedom from fear

Physiological
air, food, drink, shelter, warmth, sex, sleep

Maslow's Hierarchy of Needs

Maslow (1954) believed that the most basic level of needs must be met before an individual is motivated to aspire to the higher-level needs. Maslow referred to the bottom four levels of the pyramid as "deficiency needs" because a person does not feel anything if they are met, but can act out or become anxious if they are not. Therefore, physiological needs—such as eating, drinking, sleeping, and safety—social needs—such as friendship and sexual intimacy—self-esteem, and recognition are deficiency needs. Maslow termed the fifth level of the pyramid a "growth need" because it allows a person to strive to reach his fullest potential as a human being if he can be honest and objective with himself.

Maslow also coined the term "metamotivation" to describe the motivation of people who go beyond their basic needs and strive for something better. Maslow found that emotionally healthy individuals tend to have "peak experiences" in life, times when they might report being at their happiest, that lead to some sort of transformation (Jacobs, 2003).

Sandra Bloom (2013) takes the concept of safety as a basic need to another level. While she acknowledges the importance of physical safety, she believes that physical safety alone is not sufficient. She includes *psychological safety*—the ability to feel safe with yourself, avoiding destructive influences; *social safety*—the sense of feeling safe with others; and *moral safety*—an environment that constantly strives for integrity, responsibility, tolerance, honesty, compassion, and justice for all involved. In her work with trauma survivors, she feels that the four, non-linear key areas for organizing and addressing problems presented by troubled young people are: *safety* (attaining safety in self, relationships, and environment), *emotional management* (identifying levels of various emotions and modulating emotion in response to memories, persons, events), *loss* (feeling grief and dealing with personal losses and recognizing that all change involves loss), and *future* (trying out new roles, ways of relating and behaving as a "survivor" to ensure personal safety and help others).

Bloom (1997) created The Sanctuary Model as a blueprint for clinical and organizational change. It promotes safety and recovery from adversity through a trauma-informed community that recognizes trauma is pervasive in the experience of all human beings. It affects all involved—the young people we work with within our system, as well as the people and systems that provide services to them.

Not only does the need for feeling safe drive our behavior in terms of seeking to meet that need, it can also affect our ability to self-regulate. We are genetically wired to detect threat and danger. All sensory information that we receive from our environment is initially assessed for safety by a part of our brain called the amygdala. This happens in an instant and we are not aware of it. However, if the safety systems in the brain perceive any level of threat or danger, it triggers a neurophysiological cascade of responses that we commonly refer to as the "fight-or-flight" response. Stephen Porges (2011), a brain-body researcher at the University of Chicago believed that the brain employs a sequential series of strategies to both regulate itself and to keep us safe when faced with danger. Called Polyvagal Theory, Porges believes it is all about staying safe.

The top-level strategy is a mechanism Porges calls social engagement. It is a connecting of the social muscles of the face with the heart and is regulated through a branch of the vagus nerve. It is the most "evolved" strategy and it is used all the time to clear up misunderstandings, apologize, or get help. It acts like brakes on a car, stopping the fight-or-flight response and allowing the thinking part of our brain to work through the situation.

The next strategy is fight or flight, which is regulated by the sympathetic nervous system, allowing us to run fast or fight furiously as it shuts down non-essential systems like digestion. This system is our fallback strategy when social engagement doesn't work. At that point, or if the danger escalates, we resort to either fighting or fleeing. While effective in the short term, this response stresses the body in an extreme way. There is a third strategy if all else fails: we freeze. It is the least optimal of all strategies, but it does protect us in the case of severe injury by slowing or stopping our pain response.

It is preferable for us to operate using the social engagement strategy, as it is the least stressful position for our brains and our bodies. However, based on some young people's life experiences, their amygdalae are always in overdrive. They perceive threat and danger when there is none and/or they are unable to engage their social engagement mechanism accurately. Because of this, they are constantly at a low-level fight-or-flight response state and react or overreact to seemingly benign stimuli. They cannot access their "braking system." Essentially, they never feel totally safe even if, in reality, they are. And that makes a lot of difference in how they behave.

Story: Lizzy—Get Your Hands Off Me

Lizzy was a 16-year-old student attending an alternative academic program. At the intake meeting for the program, all that the staff was told by the parents was that she couldn't cope in the regular school system. (She'd been in four schools before finally "landing" in the alternative program.) The schools reported that while she was quite bright academically, she was argumentative and defiant. The alternative program staff reported that she was doing well in the program initially but whenever a staff member tried to talk to her about an issue or reprimand her, even gently, she would become very defensive and angry, often throwing things at staff members and leaving the building before the end of the day. Lizzy had one staff member that she seemed to be connecting with; on a particularly rough day, that staff member had been asked to see if perhaps she could spend some time with her to calm her and get her back on track. Lizzy agreed to go and see that person and as she got up to go, another staff member gently put a hand on her shoulder to guide her to the office. Lizzy whipped around, pushed the staff member violently with both hands—knocking her over—screaming, "Get your *&^$ing hands off me!" over and over. She started kicking and flailing at the person on the ground, totally out of control. It took two other staff members to pull her away and restrain her until she stopped fighting. The administration gave Lizzy a five-day suspension for fighting and hitting a staff member.

Based on what you have just read, what kind of labels might people give Lizzy? Anger issues, defiant, aggressive, oppositional, and violent all come to mind. There seems to be a history of oppositional behavior and a pattern to her way of dealing with situations that she finds somewhat stressful. But things are not always as they seem. Let's look at Lizzy's story again, but from her perspective.

Story: Lizzy—I'm Not Safe!

Lizzy was a 16-year-old student who had struggled with her peers in several schools before she ended up in the alternative program. She had witnessed severe domestic violence between her parents for as long as she could remember. It always started with her father being critical about something her mother had done or he believed had been done and ended with him grabbing her and beating her. He would then grab Lizzy and threaten her with the same treatment if she uttered a word to anyone. Last night was one of those nights. Lizzy had huddled in her bedroom, terrified and getting little sleep. When Lizzy got to school she was tired and frightened. She kept thinking about the night before and couldn't concentrate on her work. She was worried about her mother. The staff was getting frustrated with her lack of attention and they were expressing it. In her heightened state of vigilance and low-level fight-or-flight-response state, she was trying to cooperate and was going to see the staff member as requested, but physical contact triggered her amygdala into a fully-fledged fight response. She felt awful after she was able to calm down and think about things more rationally, but she was suspended, and she knew her father was not going to be happy about it. Now she was stuck at home with him for five days.

Self-Reflection 8

Can you remember a time when you didn't feel safe? Think about that time.

1) What emotions were you feeling?

_____

_____

_____

_____

2) How did you react physically?

_____

_____

_____

_____

3) What helped you get through it or over it? What calmed you down?

_____

_____

_____

_____

4) Can you imagine a situation in which the thing that helped you feel safe could make another person feel very unsafe? How would you help them feel safe?

_____

_____

_____

_____

Significant

Significance, a component of self-esteem, has to do with a feeling of being valued and cared about, the feeling that you matter to someone, which generates a sense of purpose in life. You can't "make" someone feel significant. You can try to influence it by what you say and do, by caring about someone, and by meeting their needs, but you can't be sure that the messages that you send will necessarily be received. Feeling significant is a choice everyone makes individually.

In an intensive study conducted over a period of six years, Stanley Coppersmith examined 1,748 middle-class children and their families and found that three important characteristics distinguished children with the highest self-esteem: they were more loved and appreciated at home, they had caretakers/parents who set firm guidelines, and they lived in environments that were characterized by democracy and openness. His findings, *The Antecedents of Self-Esteem*, were published in 1967. Coopersmith believed that building a healthy respect for the self was important. He also determined that the caretakers/parents of children with the highest self-esteem set clear limits and defined high standards of behavior. They "walked their talk" by modeling these tenets in their own lives.

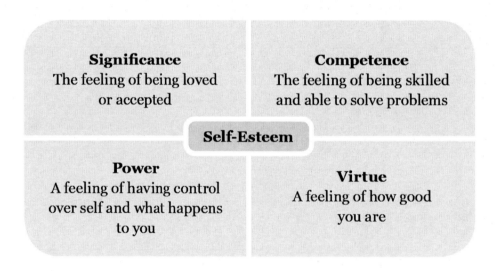

The Components of Self-Esteem: Stanley Coopersmith

Coopersmith (1967) created a four-part description of what was necessary for children to develop a positive self-image. He believed that children needed:

1. "Respectful, accepting, and concerned treatment" from parents or caretakers. This allows the child to not only accept him/herself but also to accept the values and guidance of those around him/her.
2. "A history of successes." These provide a child with a sense of reality on which to base their self-esteem.

3. "Values and aspirations." These must be personally significant and used as a measure of success.
4. "A healthy manner of responding to evaluation." A child must learn how to deal appropriately with negative evaluations of their abilities and to realize that it is possible to deal with and overcome failure.

Interestingly, while the type of parenting certainly makes a difference and the relationship between parent and child affects how pathways in the brain develop and are later acted on, a twin study at George Washington University in the 1980s found that even within the same family, every child experiences parenting in very different ways (Dunn & Plomin, 1990). This makes sense when we realize that while parents are a powerful factor in a child's life, there are many other factors involved in the shaping of how a child comes to see themselves: siblings, friends, and all those in their ecology and community.

What about failure? In some cases, today's society seems to want to protect children today from experiencing failure. Many school and community organizations have taken the try-outs and competition out of sporting activities making everyone a "winner." Adults often praise every little thing their child does, not differentiating between a poor, acceptable, or good performance. They believe that having to deal with failure or rejection will damage a child's self-esteem. We know that positive behaviors in the form of love, affection, and warmth feed mastery and self-efficacy, because when children feel safe and secure, they will explore more. The more they try and the more they explore, the more they will likely master. However, research suggests that this is not a seamless process and learning how to cope with obstacles and even failure is actually part of the healthy developmental process (Seligman, 1995). By being given multiple opportunities to try and try again in a non-critical way, we learn that failure is not the end of the road and that we are, in fact, capable of overcoming obstacles in our path and that change is possible. Children who are continually criticized or not given the opportunity to experience failure are easily frustrated and do not see change as a viable possibility. So how do we encourage the development of a feeling of significance and self-worth? Research shows that children need to have a way to measure success, opportunities to try new things and explore the world around them, the ability to deal with life's disappointments and failures, and adults that set reasonable limits and boundaries that help them understand acceptable behavior.

Story: David—I'm Invisible

David was a very quiet student who stayed to himself as much as possible. He was not into sports or hanging out with the other kids. The only thing he really liked to do was play video games on the computer. He was well-behaved and polite until he was asked to move from the computer to another activity. Then his less-than-desirable behavior was apparent. The staff was concerned that David was overly anti-social and had decided that he was missing a well-rounded repertoire of experiences, and so they were attempting to increase his socialization/interaction with other students and additional activities. While David was not thrilled about this, he was compliant in order to keep his coveted computer time. One morning, David arrived at school to see the dreaded "Out of Order" sign on the classroom computer. He asked the teacher what was going on and she told him that there was no sound, that IT had been called and would be there as soon as they could; but as they served the whole county, it could take time. David said that he could easily fix it but the teacher just smiled and told him to leave it alone. Once the IT person arrived, David was glued to the process. He kept chiming in and making repair suggestions while the IT person ignored him and the teacher kept telling him to go back to his seat. David became increasingly agitated, loudly telling anyone who would listen that all that needed to be done was to reattach the cable and set the HDMI audio device as the default. That would fix the sound problem. But everyone ignored him and finally the IT tech said it needed to go to the shop. When he left to get the paperwork, David reached into the open computer, reattached the cable, put it back together, and was inputting the correct information when the teacher caught him. She told him again to leave it alone and David exploded. He yelled, "I know what to do! That jackass didn't and none of you will listen! I'm just invisible here aren't I? Try the computer –you'll see I fixed it!" Reluctantly, the teacher turned it on: it worked like a charm. When the IT tech came back the teacher showed him it was working and had David explain what he had done, the IT tech smiled and complimented David on his trouble-shooting abilities. A ten-minute detailed conversation between David and the tech went over everyone's head, but David was animated and involved with another person.

A few days later, David was invited to the weekly IT meeting to share some of his knowledge with the techs. A whole new David emerged. He was more outgoing and interacted with other students as they talked about the things he knew. He assisted the computer teacher during class when she was swamped with questions and he started to create friendships with some of the other more tech-oriented students. Instead of feeling invisible, David finally felt accepted for himself and his ability to solve problems. He finally felt that he was significant not only in his eyes but also in the eyes of those around him.

Self-Reflection 9

1) How would you define "feeling significant"?

_____

_____

_____

_____

2) Describe one area in your life where you feel significant. How does it make you feel?

_____

_____

_____

_____

3) Is there someone in your life who has contributed to your feeling of significance? What did that person do or say to build up your self-esteem and feeling of self-worth?

_____

_____

_____

_____

4) Is there anyone in your life who made you feel insignificant? What did that person do or say that caused you to question yourself?

_____

_____

_____

_____

5) How would you help someone who didn't feel significant?

_____

_____

_____

_____

Respected

Lawrence-Lightfoot (2000) states that respect is "the single most powerful ingredient in nourishing relationships and creating a just society" (p. 13). Respect is two-dimensional. It can be shown by how we act with and around another person, or it can be felt. We can feel respected by others, or we can feel respectful of others around us. When we show respect to another person, we take their feelings, needs, thoughts, and ideas into consideration. When we respect someone, we perceive him or her as having worth and value. While there is not a lot of systematic research done on the topic of respect, those who have studied the topic feel that respect is essential in a civil society and crucial to positive human relations.

Dr. Michele Borba (2012), an educational psychologist and internationally recognized expert and author on moral development, believes that respect is a skill that must be taught because many of today's young people lack an understanding of respect. Their life experiences with respect have been minimal. They haven't seen or heard respectful interactions in their lives. She feels that there are six simple ways we can reimburse this lack of experience that allow young people to learn to be respectful.

1. **Model respectful statements**. We need to talk to our young people the way we would like them to talk to us. Remember those mirror neurons in Chapter 1? If we are not respectful to our young people, they will learn and model *disrespectful* behavior.
2. **Accentuate respect**. We need to not only be respectful of others, we need to be respectful of ourselves.
3. **Build awareness of respectful language**. As a society, we have become increasingly negative and disrespectful. The use of sarcasm, put-downs, and ridicule are becoming more and more commonplace, particularly through the use of social media. If our young people are growing up in homes where respect is not modeled, they will need to learn some additional vocabulary. Don't assume they have respectful language if they are not demonstrating it. You will need to help them brainstorm for better ways of saying things.
4. **Label appropriate respectful language**. Without prior experience, young people may not be able to tell what language is respectful and what isn't. Borba suggests using the terms "put-ups" and "put-downs" to help young people focus on statements that are appropriate and positive.
5. **Reinforce appropriate and respectful statements**. It's easier to change behavior by focusing on the positive aspects.
6. **Practice respectful behavior skills**. Young people will need this if they have not developed this prior to coming to us. As with all learning, this kind of practice is best in a natural setting. Borba reminds us that learning new behaviors is incremental and that we may need to think in "baby steps." Old habits will slowly be replaced by new and better behaviors. Don't give up. Learning new skills takes consistency and many repetitions. (Borba, 2012)

Story: Patty—You Get What You Give

I was sitting in my office one warm spring day, listening to the voices across the hall get angrier and louder. As I pushed my chair back to investigate, Patty, an outspoken 17-year-old resident, came flying through my door, screaming, "There's no way in h$ll I'll speak nicely to that bitch!" I was about to ask a question or two when a staff member came through the door behind Patty. She was furious, telling me that Patty was rude and disrespectful and would I please do something about it right now, as this kid was not speaking to her in that manner! After both Patty and the staff member had had a chance to explain their concerns, I had a resident who was refusing to be respectful because she felt that the staff member was rude to her all the time. Patty said that she would be respectful to the staff member when the staff member was respectful to her. The staff member felt that she didn't need to "earn" this young person's respect. She had always been respectful of her elders and in this case, respect came with the job title; that young lady had better watch her mouth or there would be consequences. Both people were determined that they were right and were not willing to budge.

So, I suggested we try an experiment. We agreed that nobody would use sarcasm, put-downs, personal remarks, offensive words, or negative body language (eye rolling, hands on hips, finger wagging, and so on) for 48 hours. When one spoke to the other, the one spoken to would mirror the verbal and body language in their response. We also agreed to use "I" statements instead of more accusatory "you" statements when communicating, with a liberal dose of "please" and "thank you" thrown in for good measure. It was an interesting 48 hours; when it was over, we debriefed. Patty laughed and said that she felt stupid a lot of the time with all the mirroring but that the staff member was kind of nice when she didn't have her "mean face" on, and the staff member agreed that Patty was not too bad either. They both felt that they had been treated more respectfully and that it certainly felt better than the other way. They agreed to another 48-hour practice session in the hope that this was the beginning of old habits being replaced by new and better behaviors—on both parts.

Self-Reflection 10

1) Do you think that people in your workplace are respectful enough of each other? Why or why not?

_____

_____

_____

_____

2) What are the benefits of people in the workplace (both staff and young people) treating each other with respect?

_____

_____

_____

_____

3) Do you consider yourself to be a respectful person? Why or why not? In what ways do you show respect to other adults, to the young people that you work with?

_____

_____

_____

_____

4) How is respect related to fairness?

_____

_____

_____

_____

5) Do you believe that respect is earned, not given? Explain.

_____

_____

_____

_____

Related

As humans, we are social beings. Our brains are designed to seek people in an effort to survive. Relationships are where we find our "natural habitat." Without mutually stimulating interactions, people and neurons wither and die. For human babies, survival doesn't depend on how fast they can run or how well they can hunt, but rather on the ability of their caretakers to detect the needs and intentions of those around them. For humans, other people are our primary environment (Cozolino, 2006).

When young people are successful in relationships, they will have their physiological and emotional needs met. Survival of the fittest for humans is entirely dependent on the ability to adapt to our ecology and environment. Good relationships and experiences are instrumental in the growth and development of the many systems within our brains and help us to survive well. "Optimal sculpting and development of the brain through healthy early relationships allows us to: think well of ourselves, trust others, regulate our emotions, maintain positive expectations, and utilize our intellectual and emotional intelligence in moment-to-moment problem solving" (Cozolino, 2006, p. 14).

Attachment theorists John Bowlby (1969) and Mary Ainsworth (1978) believe that every child needs a healthy attachment to caregivers who are empathetic and responsive to the child's needs. When caretakers provide environments or ecologies where there is consistent sensitivity and attunement to the needs of their children, they are providing what Bowlby called a secure base. Children can count on those caregivers for comfort and attention when they are upset. This idea was taken a step further by Ainsworth when she proposed that they also need a safe haven, or an emotionally secure place, that they can return to after any new life experience. Unfortunately, the lack of well-attuned caretakers and children who do not form secure attachments means not all children are afforded these enriched experiences.

Although early childhood attachment experiences do have a large effect on growth and development, and despite earlier scientific consensus that the brain is fixed and unchangeable by adolescence, social neuroscientists now know that the brain is changeable, or "plastic." Whenever we have an experience, neurons (the cells in our brain) fire. Every time neurons fire, there is the potential to strengthen and/or create new pathways or synapses. When neurons fire, it is even possible to stimulate the growth of new neurons that can impact future experiences. Neuroscientists call this neurogenesis. When new neurons and new pathways are created in conjunction with experience, it is called neuroplasticity. We now know our brains have a lifelong ability to restructure their neural pathways based on experience, and that any meaningful relationship can reactivate neuroplastic processes and actually change the structure of the brain (Cozolino, 2006).

Allan Schore (1994), a leading researcher in the field of neuropsychology, believes that nurturing relationships with any significant adult can play a big role in the brain's ability to change. Repeated early experiences certainly sculpt and strengthen our neural pathways, but nurturing and therapeutic relationships later in life can, to some extent, rewrite and re-sculpt the pathways laid down initially.

These therapeutic relationships and experiences can have a repairing effect and, in essence, can provide the secure emotional base and safe haven that is missing. Other significant adults in a child's life can provide open, attuned, non-judgmental experiences in a safe and secure place, and repair and reroute those early neural pathways.

Self-Reflection 11

Where does relatedness come from? It comes from groups of people organized around certain purposes—like your program. How well do you think your program relates to the young people in it? Do you think the young people in your program would agree or disagree with the following statements? Circle the one you think **they** would circle and then give reasons why they likely think that.

1) Adults in my program care about people my age. (Agree/Disagree)

_____
_____
_____
_____

2) Adults in my program listen to what I have to say. (Agree/Disagree)

_____
_____
_____
_____

3) Adults in my program don't respect what people my age think. (Agree/Disagree)

_____
_____
_____
_____

4) I trust the other kids in my program. (Agree/Disagree)

_____
_____
_____
_____

5) I trust the adults in my program. (Agree/Disagree)

_____
_____
_____
_____

We all need to feel connected and related to someone. When our life experiences have led to unmet emotional needs and a great deal of stress, it is not unusual to develop anxiety. There are five different types of developmental anxiety that can manifest themselves based on less-than-positive early experiences: *abandonment, inadequacy, guilt, conflict,* and *identity* (Wood, Quirk, & Swindle, 2007, p. 98). If young people have not been well-connected and related, the type of anxiety that can affect interactions with others is the fear of abandonment. If they fear abandonment, the need for connection becomes a priority and will dominate their behavior. If they can't find appropriate people to connect with and relate to, they will try to find artificial attachments or use unhealthy strategies for meeting those attachment needs (gang affiliation, substance abuse, sexual promiscuity, aggression, self-injury, etc.). Young people will reimburse themselves if the significant adults in their lives are not willing or available to reimburse them.

To avoid artificial attachments, we need to be sure that our young people are connected to others who are positive influences. And the more positive people they are connected to, the better! Given life's ever-changing circumstances, a huge component of having multiple connections at their disposal is the benefit of having a greater variety of resources available to them. And here is the good news: We can create new and powerful relationships and experiences with our young people. Every time we interact in a positive way with a young person is a step towards better relatedness. Seemingly little things can build into big experiences—micro interactions can yield macro results! Being present and "there" creates new experiences to help repair old painful experiences. This does, however, require trust on both parts. Many of the young people we work with are afraid that we will "abandon" them if they make a mistake or continue to repeat their early developed maladaptive patterns. By "hanging in" and being there for them, regardless of their behavior, we can prove that we are trustworthy.

Story: Chloe—Nobody Loves Me

Chloe was 17 when her teacher/counselor first met her. Reports indicated that she was oppositional, rude, and not interested in school. She was overly vigilant and very on edge. While evidently a very bright young lady, her work and attitude had been deteriorating since the school year had started. She had also begun to cut herself. Her mother had refused referral to any clinical services. By January, her behavior and performance at school had deteriorated to the point where she was suspended and referred to an off-campus alternative program. She arrived covered in scars and open cuts (arms, legs, and stomach) and an "I hate the world—and you in particular" attitude.

Initially, she would not talk to her teacher/counselor at all. She sat down, crossed her legs and arms, and stared at the teacher/counselor for days while they had a rather one-sided conversation (if that's possible). If the teacher/counselor asked her to do anything academic, she would do it, and then throw it at her or slam it on her desk; and she refused to participate in the daily group sessions. Once she decided to talk, she was verbally and emotionally abusive and tried very hard to get the teacher/ counselor to suspend her or give up on her. The teacher/counselor did her best to ignore the abuse and focus on the positive. Chloe's academics were outstanding when she chose to do her work. Still,

Chloe attended her sessions regularly and the teacher/counselor noticed over time that the cutting had stopped and most physical wounds were healing.

Chloe had been severely neglected as a child. She was an infringement on her mother's social life and was left at home to care for her younger siblings, serving as the in-house childcare provider while her mother partied and went to the bar. Mom found a live-in boyfriend and moved him into a basement suite, joining him there and leaving Chloe and her three younger brothers and sisters to fend for themselves upstairs. Chloe had been holding things together fairly well until the new boyfriend started verbally abusing her, telling her that she was useless and ugly and would never find a boyfriend. Mom was aware of what was happening but blamed Chloe. It was around that time Chloe started to cut herself and create problems at school.

Initially, Chloe needed to find someone who was supportive and who she could learn to trust. It was important for her to feel safe, but it was also helpful for her to have someone who she could relate to. Chloe and her teacher/counselor began to make the first steps towards a more transformative relationship, providing her with positive and affirming experiences with another person.

Young people express their needs in a variety of ways. They can act out, physically, aggressively, and in your face. They can also act in, where they withdraw and "check-out." Many times the act-ins are not noticed, sometimes until it is too late. Whether young people act out or act in, their needs are just as great. While we are more likely to notice the ones who act out, we also need to attend to those who act in. We all have bad days and days when our behavior is inappropriate. However, when you see young people demonstrating repeated age-inappropriate behavior, behavior that appears to be driven and persistent, or behavior that is ineffective but is displayed in all circumstances regardless of the situation or the ecology, it is a very good indicator that they are trying, albeit not in the best ways, to meet a need. Think of it as a form of communication, which, if you are on the receiving end, is most likely quite unpleasant. However, difficult behavior often occurs when young people either don't know exactly what is bothering them or when words just can't define how they perceive their situation. They can feel overwhelmed and threatened; they can feel unable to communicate their wants and needs effectively. If we think about it this way, we can understand that behavior is a symptom, not the cause; it's a hint that we need to investigate further rather than simply dealing with the behavior that we see.

Behavior and the Brain

There are four basic assumptions that underpin what we believe about behavior. They are:

- **Behavior is very complex**. It is an interaction of both physical and mental systems operating in constantly changing social and emotional environments.
- **One size does not fit all** young people with behavior issues.

- With behavior, **what you see is often not what the problem really is**. But it certainly will give you a hint as to what part of the brain is in control.
- **Behavior will change, when and only when, new pathways are created** in the brain. These new pathways will only be created by new and positive experiences.

Let's take a more in-depth look at each of these and the neuroscience that helps us understand behavior better.

"A State Becomes a Trait" or How Neural Connections Are Made

The brain consists of special cells called neurons, which are composed of several parts, including brain fibers known as dendrites. As you experience life (learn), these brain fibers grow. The fibers connect your brain cells to one another at points called synapses. The larger the brain fibers grow, the more brain cells they can connect to creating pathways. The more pathways the brain creates, the more information can be stored in your brain.

But brain fibers can only grow from existing brain fibers. In other words, to learn something new, a person must build on information that is already stored in the brain. In addition, the more a skill is practiced, the faster the connections are in the brain. This is because the regular practice of a particular skill causes the dendrites to thicken and to coat themselves with a substance called myelin, allowing information to travel more quickly from one part of the brain to another.

We are born with the most neural capability we will ever have. Based on our experiences, the brain begins to make decisions on which neural pathways to save and which need to be "pruned" away to allow for more focus to be placed on the necessary ones.

Pruning (apoptosis), occurs as our experience changes. We design our brains to meet the needs of our lives. While pruning can be a natural and necessary part of development, problems occur when too much pruning takes place in brain areas/systems that may be critical for adaptive functioning. Basically, the brain follows a "use it or lose it" principle. Pathways that we need to survive and use repeatedly will be well myelinated while the pathways that we don't use but oftentimes need, will be pruned away.

Our brains get rid of pathways that it doesn't use. It looks for the most efficient ways to do anything and avoids complex tasks if a simple one can suffice. Remember, the brain is experience dependent!

Hebb's Rule

Our brains are experience dependent but our genes play a role as well. Our genes direct the overall brain organization while experience influences how and when which genes become expressed. All aspects of an experience (sounds, smells, feelings, and so on) gather into a neural net of pathways that encodes a representation of that event. When one aspect of that net is touched by a new experience, it is likely that the whole net will be activated. We call this remembering.

The stronger the linkages within the net, the greater the chances of it being reactivated at a later date. Repetition, the emotional intensity of the experience, and myelination all strengthen the synaptic connections making up these neural pathway nets.

One-time experiences or experiences with people who don't really matter don't have that much impact, but repetition and emotional significance can create a "superhighway" of neural pathways to painful and powerful experiences. A state becomes a trait.

While myelination is mostly under genetic control, certain experiences that occur during the brain's vulnerable developmental stages can disrupt the myelination process and either worsen existing difficulties or create new challenges.

Hebb (1949) summarized this information like this: "Neurons that fire together, wire together. Neurons out of sync, fail to link."

While this all may sound a little technical, it is important to you in two ways:

1. The young people you deal with are coming to you with a set of experiences that affect their perceptions and reactions to everything around them.
2. The experiences that you bring into your program are going to affect your perceptions and reactions to the young people and adults around you.

Rigid Thinking & Irrational Beliefs

Experiences shape perception and drive behavior. Past experiences always influence new learning. Personal logic is shaped by unique life experiences and this thinking is applied fairly consistently.

A young person's sense of self is formed by repetitive interactions with significant adults and peers who provide ongoing feedback about behavior and character. This sense of self plays a central role in determining how they think about themselves, how they relates to others, and what they believe will happen in the future. It becomes a personal self-fulfilling prophecy. If a child grows up primarily with positive reinforcement, that child will internalize these experiences and see him/herself that way. If the child grows up primarily experiencing negative feedback, he/she will see him/herself in a negative light (Long, 2014).

As well as developing a sense of self from their life experiences, a child will also develop a set of beliefs about his/her world and the people encountered in that world. By elementary school age, these two sets of beliefs generally merge and are the motivating force behind the child's personality. All thoughts about life events are filtered through these belief systems. While these reality-based beliefs may start out as an accurate reflection of life experiences, they can become irrational through a process called overgeneralization. Everything gets painted with the same brush and words like "always" and "never" are applied to all events (Long, 2014).

Have you ever wondered about a young person's behavior and find yourself unable to understand why they continue to behave in this manner? You probably wonder how it makes any sense since it seems not to work for them, considering they have gotten into trouble and have been dealt consequences for the behavior. Well, actually you are wrong. It *does* work for them at some level, just one we don't understand. To our way of thinking, it doesn't work—but it does for them. Even though irrational beliefs or rigid thinking tend to operate to a child's detriment, often getting them in trouble or preventing them from seeking help when it is available, Long (2007) feels that irrational beliefs are maintained because they:

1) Provide a sense of security and control in an unstable world.
2) Allow young people to predict what will happen in future relationships.
3) Protect young people from feelings of helplessness and rage.

When young people with irrational beliefs/rigid thinking project their beliefs on those around them, they often engage adults in endless and exhausting power struggles. Their beliefs are then validated when adults respond in counter-aggressive ways.

Some irrational thinking processes become "cognitive sticking points" or mistakes in thinking that keep these young people stuck in unhealthy patterns of thinking and behaving. It is important for adults to be able to readily recognize cognitive traps as kids are employing them, so that they can disengage from the kinds of power struggles that often result from their use.

Filtering

"Black & White" Thinking

Jumping to Conclusions

Overgeneralization

Blaming

Cognitive "Sticking Points"

Filtering involves picking out a single negative detail in an incident and dwelling on it excessively. One word of criticism erases all the praise received.

Black & white thinking is polarized thinking. Things are either "black" or they are "white." People believe they have to be perfect or they are a failure, for example. There is no middle ground. People or situations are placed in "either/or" categories, with no shades of gray. The complexity of people or situations is completely ignored. If one performance falls short of perfect, they see themselves as a total failure.

Jumping to conclusions allows things to be interpreted negatively when there are no facts to support that conclusion. There are two types of conclusion jumping that can be employed. The first is "mind reading." In this case, it is arbitrarily concluded that someone is reacting negatively to them regardless of what is said or not said. The second is "fortune telling," where they assume and predict that things will turn out badly regardless of any evidence to the contrary.

Overgeneralization occurs when general conclusions are based on a single incident or a single piece of evidence. If something bad happens only once, it is expected to happen over and over again. A person may see a single, unpleasant event as part of a never-ending pattern of defeat.

Blaming means that either others are responsible for personal pain or that they blame themselves for every problem. They might say something like, "Stop making me feel bad about myself!" Nobody can "make" them feel any particular way. Only they themselves have control over their own emotions and emotional reactions. However, it is easier for them to put the blame elsewhere. What young people believe about themselves is more important in determining behavior than any facts you think that you may know about them (Long, Wood, & Fecser, 2001).

In addition to cognitive traps, young people with irrational beliefs/rigid thinking also employ one or more defense mechanisms. Defense mechanisms are used to compensate for an environmental lack, to overcome insecurity, to defend their pride, to shift the blame from themselves, to provide a self-alibi, or to retreat from a problem "with honor" and save face. Despite a nagging conscience, they justify their actions in some way or another in all cases. They are defending against the inner self with the object being the prevention of inner conflict and to feel better about their behavior. Everyone uses defense mechanisms from time to time. It is the normal way of coping under duress and if used occasionally it is not a problem. However, defense mechanisms become a problem when their repeated use stops us from eventually coming to terms with the true source of our stress.

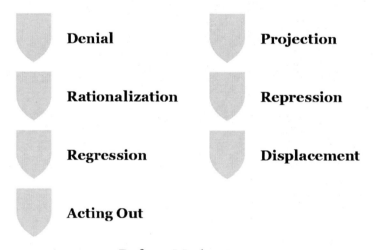

Denial	**Projection**
Rationalization	**Repression**
Regression	**Displacement**
Acting Out	

Defense Mechanisms

Denial is an outright refusal to admit or recognize that something has occurred or is currently occurring. Drug addicts or alcoholics are examples of people employing denial.

Rationalization is a defense mechanism that involves explaining an unacceptable behavior or feeling in a rational or logical manner while avoiding the true explanation for the behavior. For example, a student who blames a teacher's teaching ability for a poor mark they received on a test they didn't study for is using rationalization.

Regression occurs when people are confronted by very stressful events. During these times, they sometimes abandon coping strategies and revert to patterns of behavior used earlier in development. A relatively independent young person may becoming clingy or resort again to bedwetting.

Acting-out involves performing an extreme behavior in order to express thoughts or feelings the person feels incapable of otherwise expressing. Instead of saying, "I'm angry with you," a person who acts out may instead throw a book at the person or punch a hole through a wall. When a person acts out, it can function as a pressure release, often helping the individual feel calmer and peaceful again. A child's temper tantrum is a form of acting out when he or she doesn't get his or her way with a parent. Self-injury may also be a form of acting-out, expressing in physical pain what they cannot bear emotionally.

Projection is shifting unacceptable thoughts, feelings, and impulses within oneself onto someone else, so that those same thoughts, feelings, beliefs, and motivations are perceived as being possessed by the other. An example of this happens when one person tells another that they never listen to them, when they themselves, in fact, were the ones not listening.

Repression is the unconscious blocking of unacceptable thoughts, feelings, and impulses. The key issue with repression is that people do it unconsciously, so they often have very little control over it.

Displacement involves taking out our frustrations, feelings, and impulses on people or objects that are less threatening. If a young person has had a tough night at home and comes into their program and takes it out on the staff instead of the people that caused them the grief, this is an example of displacement.

There are other types of cognitive traps and defense mechanisms but they all serve the same purpose. They start out as a form of protection from feelings of anxiety that have surfaced because the individual feels threatened in some way; these can frequently become young people's "go-to" behavior because their experiences have given them no other options.

The Triune Brain

Earlier we said that while behavior did not necessarily help us understand why someone was behaving in a particular way, it would help us understand what part of the brain was in control. This is good information to have because how we respond changes dramatically from one part of the brain to another.

Paul McLean's Triune Brain is a broad representation of basic brain systems. There are more than three systems that work together to help us to exist, but for now, we will look at three: *survival*, *emotional*, and *logical brain* systems. They have separate functions but are designed to work together. During development, the brain organizes itself from the bottom up—from the least complex to the most complex areas. While significantly interconnected, each of the regions of the brain mediates distinct functions. At birth, the brainstem areas responsible for regulating cardiovascular and respiratory function must be intact for the infant to survive.

As the brain develops, the process is influenced by a host of neurotransmitters, neurohormones, and neuromodulator signals. These signals help target cells migrate, differentiate, sprout dendritic trees, and form synaptic connections. These crucial neural networks originate in the lower brain areas and project to every other part of the developing brain. This allows these systems the unique capacity to communicate across multiple regions simultaneously and therefore provide an organizing and orchestrating role during development later in life. Impairment in the organization and functioning of these systems can result in a cascade of dysfunction from the lower regions up to all the target areas higher in the brain. This can disrupt normal development. Impairment can occur in utero through the use of drugs and/or alcohol by the mother during pregnancy or in early childhood through neglect or trauma.

Briefly, the brain systems can be described as follows:

The **survival brain** is our life support system (breathing/heartbeat/temperature control). It develops in utero and is a non-thinking, purely reactive system. Its job is to recognize potential threats and danger and react to them with fight, flight, or freeze behavior.

The **emotional brain** or limbic area, assigns positive and negative values to life events. Emotions motivate behavior by adding meaning and intensity to memories and preparing us for action. We know now that this is not the only area where emotions are processed; the frontal lobe and other regions are also activated, and some limbic structures like the hippocampus are involved in non-emotional processes such as memory.

The **logical brain** is our thinking brain. The frontal lobe comprises the rational and executive control center of the brain, processing higher-order thinking and directing problem-solving. In addition, one of the most important functions of this part of the brain is to use cognitive processing to monitor and control the emotions generated by the limbic area.

Amygdala War: The Survival Brain in Control

Nestled between both the survival brain system and the emotional system is a tiny almond-shaped structure located deep in the medial temporal lobe (you actually have two—one in each hemisphere of the brain). It is essential for us to have the ability to feel certain emotions and to perceive them in other people. This includes fear and the many changes that it causes in the body. If, for example, you are being followed at night by a shady-looking character, you are afraid, and your heart is pounding, chances are that your amygdala is very active.

The amygdala modulates all of our reactions to events that are important for our survival. Events that warn us of imminent danger are therefore very important stimuli for the amygdala, as are events that signal the presence of food, sexual partners, and competition. The amygdala plays a protective role by letting us react almost instantaneously to the presence of danger. This reaction happens so quickly that we are often startled at first, and only afterward are we aware of what it was that frightened us.

Many times, the young people we work with are filled with prior experiences that have been threatening or actually involved issues of survival, which is why they may be overly sensitive to the day-to-day events that most of us take for granted. Because of this sensitivity, they are often quick to engage in powerful survival strategies that have been historically useful in stopping others or situations from becoming a problem. Their amygdala remains in an over-active state and makes them prone to overreacting behavior (overt aggression, passive aggression, yelling, violently posturing, etc.) These are attempts to divert a real or perceived threat. If these types of behavior do not result in the diversion of the perceived threat or make the adult involved go away, these young people will then resort to engaging them by arguing and fighting with them. When this type of engagement occurs with another person, we have what our NeuroRelational Framework terms "an amygdala war."

This takes place when two people become entangled with one another and their two survival systems are actively "fighting," one trying to overpower the other and reduce the threat. These engagements are counterproductive because they are simply utilizing the most primitive systems in our brain. These systems only react—no thinking is taking place. When we have two reactive individuals, we have two non-thinking individuals who set the stage for a powerfully negative outcome. An understanding of this part of the brain will help you recognize the early signs of a young person attempting to engage in an amygdala war, and allow you instead to utilize your logical/cognitive strength to diffuse and deflect the engagement.

If the survival brain system is in control, remember that this brain system only reacts. It cannot think or have a rational discussion. First and foremost, you need to calm the young person and possibly the ecology as well. It is important to be attuned to and manage sensory input in the environment that could cause a re-escalation like sounds, smells, sights, or touches. Do whatever you can to calm the brain/body. It might mean just sitting with the young person and waiting, or it could mean listening to their complaints and validating them. At this point you are only moving towards a readiness to talk. This process can take a while as the body can take 30 to 45 minutes to come out of flight-or-fight mode fully.

Cognitive Combat: The Logical Brain in Control

The emotional brain also receives input from and can be controlled by the thinking brain. The human cerebral cortex (the logical brain) is the part of the brain at the front of our heads that sets us apart from all other animals. This part of the brain is responsible for cognition and plays an essential role in perception, memory, thought, intellect, and consciousness. The cerebral cortex provides impulse control, decision-making, and assists in the prediction of future outcomes. It helps to modulate our emotions, body movement, and general behavior. People who have not had a normal course of development will respond differently in these areas because appropriate people have not been involved in their lives, ultimately creating the thinking systems within the brain differently than those who have had typical development.

Like an excavator used on a construction site, the cerebral cortex can "dig" into the brain and pull up information from other parts of the brain to help us make decisions by consolidating bits and pieces of information based on survival and emotional experiences in our past. However, the brain is only able to dig down and retrieve what is there. If a young person's life has been filled with stress, abuse, or trauma, the brain can only retrieve those types of memories. When a young person's life has had a more balanced experience of both good and bad, then his/her brain has more choices in its "file cabinet of life." Having more choices means more potential outcomes. More potential outcomes provide more opportunities to have the right coping skill to apply to the scenario needing attention. Because of this unique ability, humans often seek people with more experience in certain areas of life and especially those who can put the bits and pieces together in a clear, concise, and easily understood manner to assist them during difficult times. Logical brains can be shaped by anything and anyone. So, looking at the logical approaches a young person takes towards life often tells us much about his or her experiences and what has worked or not worked. The logical brain cannot ignore emotions, but it does try to help make sense of them and learn to regulate them better in life. When we ask someone to think logically, they can only draw on their existing "files." Logic is based on experience, so what can be quite illogical to one person (if he or she is lacking experiences) can make perfect sense to someone else.

Many challenging young people have mastered the art of using their logical systems to engage adults in something we identify as cognitive combat. This is an attempt by the young person to engage an adult in a war of intellect, words, or manipulative scenarios. It is when both the young person and the adult are "locked" in a battle between logical brains, based on their experiences that have shaped their own personal logic. This use of cognitive combat can either be intentional or unintentional. The primary marker is that the logical brain is in play, where thoughts, planning, and strategies are utilized in an attempt to gain power, status, or control over people or the environment. Neurologist and neuropsychiatrist Richard Restack (2006) identifies this as an attempt for two people to intentionally try to mentally outperform the other in a negative way.

When looking at cognitive combat, it is important to remember that we are a product of our experiences. Not all logic demonstrated by young people makes sense to us. In fact, we may even describe it as "illogical" from our own perspective. We have to keep in mind that we are looking at their behavior through our perspective until we have gained insight into theirs. These illogical behavioral demonstrations are frequently a young person's way of trying to say something simple such as "get away from me," "stop trying to help me; I feel worthless," or "I need something and don't know how to tell you." We must recognize the early signs of cognitive combat and refuse to engage with a young person at this level. If we do engage, the young person walks away with a more solidified experience of another adult who "fights" with them or who refuses to take their perspective. This non-therapeutic type of interaction fails to reimburse young people with new, positive experiences. To be fully in the moment with them, adults need to listen to their words, watch their behavior, and ask them about their life stories to determine how to support them NeuroDynamically. With this experiential knowledge, we become empowered to maximize our opportunities to sculpt their experiences into constructive memories.

If the logical brain system is in charge, young people are capable of rational discussion and will need very little calming. Consider the emotional state that is producing the behavior. If they were sad, you would likely see withdrawal or tears, whereas if they were angry you might see aggressive fighting behaviors and/or swearing. Keep in mind that the personal logic they will be using is based on their personal experience. It may seem rational or irrational to you, but you need to consider what experiences have contributed to the style of thinking being exhibited. Then ask yourself: what new experiences are needed? And finally, how can you play a role in reshaping their experiences and retraining their behavior?

Can We Talk? Changing Rigid Thinking and the Brain

The brain is neuroplastic. That means it has the capacity to change and rewire itself in response to the stimulation of learning and experience throughout our lifetime. Learning increases connections between neurons, increases cellular metabolism, and increases the production of nerve growth factor, a substance produced by the body to help maintain and repair neurons. For most of history, scientists believed that once a person reached adulthood their mental abilities were set for life. Decades of research, however, have established that the brain's abilities are malleable and constantly change in response to experience. New behaviors and even some environmental changes or physical injuries have been shown to stimulate the brain to create new neural pathways or reorganize existing ones, altering how we process information.

It is believed that in repeating an activity, the brain tends to fall back on the same set of existing neural pathways. To continue developing, the brain must be exposed to novel experiences that challenge it to adapt and work in new ways.

The Brain and Talk Therapy

If you were to look at a brain physically, you would find two distinct divisions split down its middle into a right hemisphere and a left hemisphere. These hemispheres communicate with each other through a thick band of an amazing 200 to 250 million nerve fibers called the corpus callosum, along with smaller bands of fibers called commissures. While the hemispheres are similar—what one side has so does the other—they also have areas of specialization. Each hemisphere appears to be specialized for some behaviors and functions and has developed to perceive life experiences uniquely.

The primary duty of the right side of the brain is to control muscles on the left side of the body, while the left side of the brain controls muscles on the right side of the body. Also, in general, sensory information from the left side of the body crosses over to the right side of the brain and information from the right side of the body crosses over to the left side of the brain.

In humans, the left hemisphere is usually the dominant one of the two and is biased towards analytical and sequential thinking. While both hemispheres are responsible for aspects of language function, most of the specialized language areas are found in the left hemisphere. The left hemisphere is dominant for instructing us how to consciously cope and problem solve. It focuses and elaborates on detail by incorporating logic and concreteness into our thinking patterns. The left hemisphere is critical in helping to produce explanations of our experiences by decoding details and organizing them into understandable events. When we are able to make sense of the events that take place in our lives, we are able to predict and plan more effectively and efficiently. The left hemisphere appears to be associated with details and information.

The right hemisphere is biased in the control of emotion, bodily experience, and processes that are out of our voluntary control (Devinsky, 2000). It specializes in receiving and analyzing information from the outside world, especially those social cues received from the verbal and nonverbal behavior of others. It appraises safety and danger, helping us to decide whether to approach or avoid specific individuals and situations. The right hemisphere also appears to be dominant for facial recognition, visual imagery, body awareness, and socio-emotional information. The right hemisphere provides a more global perspective. It helps us to make sense of other people, our social relationships, and ourselves. The right hemisphere helps us connect how we "feel" about our life experiences and guides us in our decision-making, especially dealing with those things that we might want to avoid in life.

Healthy brains are integrated brains. Integration occurs when the left and right hemispheres are working in collaboration with each other and information is being exchanged efficiently between both hemispheres through the corpus callosum. Integration of the hemispheres allows us to be flexible in how we think and to self-regulate our behavior (Badenoch, 2008; Siegel, 2007). Failure to connect and attune with others tends to lead to rigid and or chaotic ways of thinking. When adults are acting in a therapeutic way, they are attuning by connecting with challenging young people via their right brains. In essence, connection takes place in and between people's right hemispheres. Since the right brain assists us in understanding our personal stories, the left brain adds the needed details to make sense of the various experiences since birth. These experiences have shaped the neural structures within the brain and have resulted in the design of specific behavioral patterns that have adapted to the people and world around them. When the hemispheres of the brains of young people are not integrated, they are heavily influenced by one hemisphere and become stuck and unable to see multiple perspectives. They may become overly reliant on strategies that do not work—yet they keep using them over and over. Life might be experienced as too rigid and concrete (left hemisphere) or too uncertain, disorganized, or unpredictable (right hemisphere). Proper integration is crucial in the healing process. We must use our left brain to identify strategies and support that will help our young people while accessing our right brains to connect and relate to them in a meaningful and genuine manner.

Chapter 4

Chaos, Stress, & Trauma-Informed Care

· ·

It's not the load that breaks you down, it's the way you carry it. Lou Holt

Stress, Chaos, & Trauma

Understanding the impact of stress, chaos, and trauma on the developing brain is extremely important. Each of these plays critical roles in shaping the developing brain in ways that help to adapt to challenging environments. In essence, brains change to survive and behaviors develop as a result.

Chaos is a term typically used within the constructs of psychology to "describe environments that are characterized by high levels of noise, crowding and instability, as well as a lack of temporal and physical structuring (few regularities, routines, or rituals; nothing has its time or place)" (Evans & Wachs, p. 5, 2010). Other researchers in this field have added additional environmental dimensions, such as the quality of the neighborhood, noise, inadequate supervision, multiple caregivers and multiple homes, employment issues, and fear and uncertainty. While this list is not all-inclusive, note that the focus here is on the effect of chaotic environments on child development.

Stress, as described by endocrinologist Hans Selye in the 1930s, was originally used describe physiological responses in lab animals. He later broadened and popularized the term to include the perceptions and responses of humans trying to adapt to the challenges of everyday life. Used broadly, stress ranges from mild irritation to severe problems that result in a breakdown of health. In popular usage, it would include almost any event or situation between these extremes. Signs of stress can be cognitive, emotional, physical, or behavioral.

Trauma is used to describe experiences or situations that are emotionally painful and upsetting. They may or may not be extraordinary events, but the key to something being a trauma is that whatever the event, it overwhelms the person's ability to cope, leaving them feeling completely powerless.

Keeping these definitions in mind, let's look at each one in more detail.

Chaos and Disorder

A chaotic home environment has a profound impact on a child's well-being and development. Growing up in a chaotic environment has been shown to have a negative impact on academic, behavioral, and self-regulatory outcomes (Martin, Razza, & Brooks-Gunn, 2011). Chaotic environments can disrupt the brain's development and stress response system, putting impacted children at risk of chronic diseases later in life (Miller, Vhen, & Fok, 2009). In fact, Gary Evans (2006) an environmental and developmental psychologist from Cornell University has found that the impact of the physical environment is as significant in child development as parental and peer influence.

A chaotic environment has been linked to the following outcomes:

- lower academic achievement (Hart et al., 2007)
- poorer cognitive and communication skills (Evans & Wach, 2010)
- poorer reading and language skills (Maxwell & Evans, 2000)
- short- and long-term attention problems (Landhuis, Pouton, Welch, & Hancox, 2007)
- behavior problems (Ackerman et al., 1999)
- anxiety, depression, and aggression (Kirkorian et al., 2009)
- lower effortful control (self-regulation) (Valinente, Lemery-Chalfant, & Reiser, 2007)
- less ability to learn and use effective coping mechanisms like self-soothing (Evans, 2006)

In addition, chaotic environments impact parenting behaviors, producing:

- less optimal parenting behaviors (Matheny et al., 1995)
- parents being less responsive and attentive to children (Kirkorian et al., 2009)
- less expression of warmth and harsher discipline methods (Coldwell, Pike, & Dunn, 2006)
- less supportive parenting (Miner & Clarke-Stewart, 2008)

While different types of chaos affect each of these outcomes, the reason why chaos is harmful to child development comes from what Urie Bronfenbrenner called the "proximal process". Simply put, the proximal process means that everything we learn from birth onwards, we learn from imitating the people around us. We learn to talk, we pick up habits, and we gain insights into life from the people in our ecologies. For the process of the proximal process to be effective, it has to occur regularly, over a period of time, and interactions become progressively and increasingly more complex. This is why chaos is so problematic. Chaotic environments are not regular or predictable, and, because of this unpredictability, are not able to sustain a progressive complexity of interactions. Interactions between child and adult are shortened and are unpredictable and irregular, so a child growing up in a chaotic environment cannot develop meaningful relationships as predictability and regularity of interactions with caregivers are needed for this to happen (Bronfenbrenner & Evans, 2000).

One important note: most research on chaos and development statistically controlled for socio-economic status. While poverty can breed chaotic conditions, chaos is not directly equated to poverty (Evans et al., 2005). Not all children living in poverty experience the chaotic conditions that negatively impact development.

How Chaos Rewires the Brain

Recalling Hebb's rule, remember that neurons that "fire together wire together." Growing up in a chaotic environment can cause a brain to develop well-established, easily accessed pathways that produce behaviors and coping strategies that are counterintuitive in non-chaotic environments. It can also cause the brain to develop in a dysregulated manner (neural structures get "out of whack") in part because of a brain structure called the hippocampus.

The hippocampus is a horseshoe-shaped structure adjacent to the amygdala. Like the amygdala, the hippocampus is a paired structure with mirror-image halves in the left and right sides of the brain. The hippocampus has several functions, but one of its most important seems to be its role in the formation of new memories about experiences in life. Research into the role of the hippocampus suggests that during wakefulness the hippocampus receives input from other parts of the brain involved in the initial encoding of an experience and binds this information into a memory. This memory is then transferred to the neocortex during sleep where it is stored and integrated within pre-existing memories. This process can take up to a year or more. While some memory transfer occurs when we are awake, most happens largely during sleep, where the hippocampus "replays" the bits and pieces of the experience, embedding them deeper and deeper into the brain until they are more or less permanent (Carter, 1998). Until this happens, the hippocampus is needed to retrieve and put that memory in the context of the different bit and pieces of the memory until it is fully encoded or stored. The hippocampus also assesses experiences to determine if they are threatening or neutral. If the hippocampus perceives the experience as neutral, it sends a message to the amygdala to stop the stress response (LeDoux, 1996; Van der Kolk, 1996). The hippocampus is very susceptible to the chemicals produced when stress or threat is perceived.

Despite the type of chaos, the brain perceives it as low-level stress. In most cases, it does not trigger a fight-or-flight response but it will produce stress hormones. If these hormones are produced on a regular basis, they affect the hippocampus, causing it to shrink in volume. This structural remodeling affects the ability to store memories and store them correctly and alters behavioral responses. While this can be frustrating for those who work with young people coming from chaotic backgrounds, neuroplasticity is our friend. Just as the pathways in the brain were developed because of early experiences, new pathways can be created by new, more positive experiences.

Story: Jake—It's Just Too Quiet Here

Jake was a 15-year-old in a new foster placement. He had been placed with a family that had fostered many high-tier boys with severe behavior and adjustment issues. The dad was pleased to see that Jake seemed to be fitting in seamlessly. He was very compliant, polite, studious, well behaved at school, and fitted in well with the other boys in the family. One day, as dinner was being prepared, Dad noticed that Jake was agitated and pacing, which was very unusual. If he had something on his mind, he usually said something and often did his talking around meal prep, so Dad asked Jake if there was something bothering him. Jake wheeled around and screamed, "It's too f*cking quiet! It is so f*cking quiet!" Dad was shocked. Jake rarely swore or had outbursts like the one he had just witnessed. Dad stopped and looked around. There was no noise. In fact, the house was like it always was. He looked at Jake as Jake screamed, "I can't live here anymore!" Dad took a breath and calmly asked Jake what he meant. Jake responded, "I can't concentrate. There's no music. There's nobody here to talk to. There's no music. There is no one sitting on the porch to socialize with and there's no music." After much discussion and lots of questions, it became apparent that Jake had come from a very chaotic home. There was loud music playing constantly and people coming and going all hours of the day and night. Jake's brain was used to loud music and the quiet environment that the family took for granted was so foreign to Jake that he felt extremely uncomfortable. He needed his music. After some brainstorming, Jake was given the opportunity to wear headphones and listen to his music as loudly as he wanted to. A win-win: Jake got what he needed, was fine with his placement, and the family was not disrupted by music playing night and day.

You have just read about how chaos rewires the brain. In Jake's situation, his brain was used to the noise, the people, and the music. When he moved to his foster placement, he experienced a "culture shock." He had arrived in a quiet, non-chaotic home. Dad had wisely realized that the placement was not the issue when Jake kept focusing on the lack of music. He noted that the environmental change was huge for Jake. His brain was not used to the quiet that they considered normal. While he had been over-stimulated in his own home, he was seriously under-stimulated in the placement home and his amygdala was telling him something was wrong. Jake's low-level stress was producing stress hormones making him agitated and so uncomfortable that he just wanted to get out of there. By being attuned to Jake's prior experiences and letting him wear the headphones, Dad averted what could have become a full-blown placement crisis. Interestingly, Jake only wore the headphones for a few days.

Stress and the Brain

A young person's brain appraises everything that they experience. Their senses send information to the thalamus, the router of all information in the brain. It simultaneously relays the information to both the prefrontal cortex and the amygdala. This gives them two possible ways to process their experiences: the "low road" or the "high road" (LeDoux, 1996). Their brain uses the low road, from the thalamus directly to the amygdala, when survival depends on a purely reactive, non-thinking response. The thalamus makes a quick decision: is it good or bad, threatening or non-threatening? Meanwhile, the cortex also receives this sensory information and begins to process it. The brain compares it to other experiences in its files and this information is forwarded to the emotional brain. The emotional brain assigns an emotional tag to the experience. This message from the amygdala is then relayed to the hypothalamus and the motor regions of the brain, resulting in a physical response. This all happens in a fraction of a second and involves unconscious brain processes (Damasio, 1994).

When a threat or stressor is realized and the brain signals the body to begin preparing for flight or fight, a part of the brain called the hypothalamic-pituitary-adrenal (HPA) system is activated. The HPA system triggers the production and release of steroid hormones (glucocorticoids), including the primary stress hormone cortisol (Sapolsky, Romero, & Munck, 2000). Cortisol is very important in organizing systems throughout the body (including the heart, lungs, circulation, metabolism, immune systems, and skin) to deal quickly with an impending threat (Miller, Chen, & Zhou, 2007). The HPA system also releases certain neurotransmitters (chemical messengers) called catecholamines, particularly dopamine, norepinephrine, and epinephrine (adrenaline). Catecholamines activate the amygdala, which triggers an emotional response to a stressful event (Sapolsky, 2004; Sapolsky, Romero & Munck, 2000). Adrenaline is produced and the secretion of cortisol is activated in the adrenal cortex. Your heartrate and breathing increase; your blood pressure and blood sugar rise; and your immune response is suppressed.

During a stressful event, catecholamines also suppress activity in areas at the front of the brain concerned with short-term memory, concentration, inhibition, and rational thought. This sequence of mental events allows a person to react to the threat quickly and respond with one of the five Fs (fight, flight, freeze, feed, or fornicate—although usually it is one of the first three options). A preoccupation with the threat reduces a person's ability to make good decisions or engage in other complex cognitive process.

Stress is only intended to be a short-term solution to a threat. It gets you moving and out of harm's way or it motivates you to respond. Stress activators and modulators play significant roles in preparing the mind, and most specifically the body, for response to an overwhelming situation. They also cause inflammation in the body. Prolonged stress begins to impact vital body organs and systems in a negative way. In fact, cortisol has been linked to a variety of health problems and dysfunction, including damage to the prefrontal cortex and hippocampus.

Stress and Pressure: Good and Bad

As strange as it sounds, there is such a thing as good stress (eustress). In the short term, some stress or pressure provides immediate strength that can act to motivate and inspire us. One example of this is when athletes flood their bodies with fight-or-flight adrenaline to power an explosive performance. Another example is when deadlines are used to motivate people who seem unmotivated or those who are having difficulty getting started on the task at hand.

However, too much stress is a bad thing (distress). For example, a demanding boss at work who creates unreasonable demands and deadlines will create distress in employees. In these situations, stress responses cause our performance to suffer. In the NeuroRelational Framework, we use the concept of stress becoming too much for a person when pressures are greater than the available internal or external resources. This stress formula would be written as follows:

Stress = Pressures > Resources (S = P > R)

According to Daniel Goleman, when people are under stress, brain function moves on a continuum from the slower, logical, thought-processing pre-frontal cortex towards the quick-moving amygdala in the midbrain—the fight-or-flight survival zone. In 1908, Robert Yerkes and John Dodson classified this idea as a continuum that can be represented by an "upside-down U with its legs spread out a bit" (Goleman, 2006).

The Tipping Point

The Yerkes-Dodson Law explains the relationship between levels of stress (arousal) and mental performance such as learning or decision-making. Too little stress (hypostress) leads to boredom. As the level of stress increases, an individual can move upward on the "U" through levels of attention and motivation until maximum cognitive efficiency is reached. This "tipping point" differs from individual to individual.

As the challenge, or stressor, increases past this tipping point (hyperstress), it will exceed an individual's ability to handle the stress. Performance and learning begin to suffer as the amygdala function debilitates the prefrontal activity. Progressively, the brain's executive center loses control of the ability to think through situations. As the pressure intensifies, people are less able to "learn, hold information in working memory, to react flexibly and creatively, to focus attention at will, and plan and organize effectively... what neuroscientists call cognitive dysfunction" (Goleman, 2006, p. 268). This is made worse when the neural circuitry from the amygdala runs to the right side of the pre-frontal cortex, causing people to fixate on the cause of the stress. This fixation undermines the capacity for additional learning and makes the generation of new ideas impossible. Essentially, it "hijacks" attention. In addition, anxiety or stress causes the brain to secrete high levels of the stress hormone cortisol and the neuroreceptor norepinephrine, causing further interference with the processes for learning and memory.

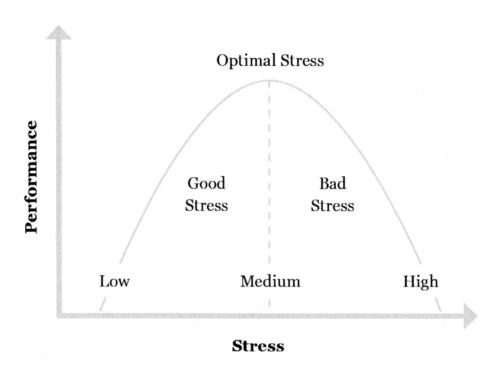

Yerkes-Dodson Law

Learning and memory are impacted because the hippocampus is damaged by prolonged exposure to cortisol. This exposure both reduces the existing number of neurons and slows the rate at which new neurons are added. In effect, it shrinks the overall volume of the hippocampus. However, the good news is that this is not a permanent state, just as it wasn't with chaos. Once the stress is dealt with, the hippocampus regains neurons and returns to its original size (Elizinga & Roelofs, 2005). While cortisol impairs the hippocampus, it stimulates the amygdala. This causes us to focus on how we feel instead of what is actually going on, and it is this emotional response that we will remember (Goleman, 2006).

Balance is critical. We need a little stress in life. If we lack the necessary levels of pressure to do things, we will suffer. However, persistent stress that is not resolved through coping or adaptation is not good for us either. The difference between which experiences will cause eustress or distress is determined by the disparity between a person's resources to cope and his or her personal expectations.

Strategy Sheet 2: Strategies to Reduce Stress

You can reduce stress by:

A. **Giving young people opportunities for personal control and decision-making**. A residential program for young offenders (adolescents and young adults) had an interesting way of giving their young people an opportunity to be involved in decisions about their behavior. They called it the "3 Ms." The Ms were for *mistake, mischief,* and *mayhem*. The first time a resident violated a rule, they went to a supervised room to talk to a staff member about their behavior. It was logged as their first M, and the assumption was that for whatever reason, a *mistake* had been made and after the allowed amount of time they returned to program activities. If a rule violation happened again that day, the second M was logged as *mischief* and the discussion looked very different. This time, it was assumed there was intent and the young person was reminded that if they got their third M—*mayhem*—it would be considered intentional and restrictions would occur. The residents were all aware of this system and they had two choices: either alter their behavior or make a choice to be restricted. It put the responsibility for their behavior in their hands, rather than in the hands of the staff. The residents had a certain level of control and the staff heard less blaming if the third M occurred.

B. **Share the power when you can**. Feeling a sense of power helps young people feel that they have some control over their lives. It also helps them to feel significant and related. A sense of power is fundamentally related to the development of an internal locus of control. If young people feel that they do not have any power, common reactions include becoming: withdrawn, passive-aggressive, rebellious, and/or hostile.

C. **Offer predictability through overviews, routines, rituals, and reviews**. The brain welcomes routine as a sign of comfort, stability, and familiarity. Routines represent these things and the people we associate with the most. They help us with the social connection process that is so vital to our brain. Ceremonies, routines, and rituals help us understand others' cultures and experiences to make connections and establish trust. The same residential justice program that used the 3M system had a special ritual called "The Bear Award." The school mascot was a stuffed bear with very funky sunglasses; he went to every assembly and on every field trip. Each day, the staff was charged with the task of catching their residents doing something right or good. (What a nice way to focus on strengths instead of deficits.) The next morning, each student that had been spotted would be called down to the office. There they were congratulated by a staff member and received a Bear Award certificate, detailing what they had done. They could then go to a blank chart on the wall (the squares were numbered across the top and alphabetized down the side) and sign their name in an empty square. At the end of the month, five squares were randomly drawn and the residents who had written their name in those squares were treated to a pizza lunch with the administrator. I stood and watched one morning as the awards were given out. The age of the young people made no difference. Each and every one of them was proud of their award and pleased to be noticed by the staff.

D. **Help young people find positive outlets for their frustrations**. Meditation, exercise/working out, relaxation techniques, and yoga are all good stress relievers. Humor and laughter are also helpful. Laughter has been found to soothe tension, relax the body, improve immune function, increase personal satisfaction, and improve mood by lowering cortisol (a stress hormone) and increasing endorphin production in the brain.

E. **Reinforce the belief that conditions can and will improve despite temporary setbacks**. Setbacks are a normal part of everyone's life. We all make mistakes and hopefully use them as an opportunity to learn from them. By allowing young people to realize that mistakes and setbacks aren't the end of the world, we help them become more resilient. Resilience is an *application* not a characteristic and is based in positive transformation experiences. It is the ability to bounce back, to properly adapt to stress and adversity by flexibly applying the necessary skills. Many of our young people have resilience, street smarts for example, but need to add to their repertoire. Our job is to connect with them and help them add skills like: the ability to make realistic plans; the capability of taking the necessary steps to follow through with plans; the development of communication and problem-solving skills; and the ability to manage strong impulses and feelings.

F. **Role model good stress support and problem-solving skills.** It's those mirror neurons again. Children and young people learn various responses by watching what others do in similar situations. Mirror neurons coordinate the neurological mechanisms that record these responses. Later, we imitate the responses. The implication here is twofold: if we don't remain calm and in control ourselves, our young people 1) learn that this is how to handle stress and 2) will respond to us in the same manner.

Fear Regulation

Our ability to control our actions is not innate. It emerges as we develop, and it is necessary for positive social relations and successful learning. Emotional self-control appears to play a role in child resiliency and later adjustment; young people that do not learn self-control in preschool can become bullies with aggressive habits of interaction that create problems for the people around them.

The brain's frontal lobe plays a big part in monitoring the limbic area in an effort to keep emotions under control. The part of the frontal lobe that appears to be closely involved in monitoring emotions is called the anterior cingulate (AC). The AC becomes highly activated under a variety of circumstances such as: whenever someone attempts to resolve conflicting ideas; or if they face distress; or if they are fearful. When disagreements arise that can't seem to be resolved, the brain feels distress, and this prompts the amygdala to generate negative emotions that can escalate unless some mechanism intervenes to provide restraint. In these situations, it is the job of the AC to rein in the amygdala, thereby tempering the expression of distress. If we can do that successfully, the prefrontal cortex (the thinking part of the brain) takes control and logically sorts out the "danger" being faced. If the internal conflict cannot be resolved, the amygdala takes control and activates the fight-or-flight response as the "danger" is viewed as insurmountable.

Losing Self-Control

Young People

Just as our ability to control our self-regulation is not innate, the rules for exhibiting self-control are not innate either. They also need to be learned. Brain mechanisms like the anterior cingulate are there to help process incoming information and generate responses. But, it is up to the individual to learn and decide which response is appropriate for each situation.

There are four primary reasons that cause young people to lose control: childhood environment, age, stress, and brain damage or deficits (Sousa, 2009). Here are some questions to consider when determining whether or not young people truly do not understand how and why to self-regulate in a situation, or whether they are simply choosing not to.

1. **Is loss of control a frequent occurrence?** We all do it when there is enough provocation. But is it the norm rather than the exception?
2. **What did they learn about self-control in the home?** How do parents deal with misbehavior? How do parents model responses to difficult situations—show restraint or fly off the handle? What, if any, are the consequences of losing control?
3. **Brain maturation**. Are they physically capable of showing restraint? Generally speaking, the younger the child, the greater the overreaction. The brain matures from bottom to top

and back to front. Thousands of years of learning have taught the brain that survival and emotional messages have high priority when filtering through all the incoming signals from the body's senses. We know that the emotional regions of the brain develop faster and mature much earlier than the frontal lobes (the thinking brain). The limbic area is fully mature around the ages of 10 to 12 years, but the frontal lobes mature closer to 22 to 24 years of age. Consequently, the emotional system is more likely to win the tug of war for control of behavior during the pre-adolescent and adolescent years. Emotional messages guide young persons' behavior, including directing their attention to a learning situation. Young people are likely to respond emotionally to a situation much faster than rationally and that often gets them into trouble. For example, if two young people bump into each other in the hall, they are more likely to punch than apologize. EMOTIONAL ATTENTION COMES BEFORE COGNITIVE RECOGNITION.

4. **Are they under continual stress, unsafe conditions, unrealistic expectations, bullying?** If so, cortisol may be impacting their hippocampus and amygdala.

5. **Neurotransmitter imbalances** can cause the interruption of nerve signals that prevent the loss of emotional control. A congenital defect or damage to the anterior cingulate or mirror neuron system causes similar problems. This may be an area to be explored if nothing else is working (Sousa, 2007).

Adults

Unlike young people, adults generally are capable of understanding why and how to self-regulate. However, there are six factors that can interfere with that ability and derail an adult's ability to exert control: being in a bad mood; feeling helpless; the violation of personal values; feeling embarrassed or uncomfortable; personal triggers; and personal stress (Long, 1995). As adults, we need to be aware of these factors, and be sure that we do not let them override our logical brains.

When adults ignore the impact of stressful events and blame kids for their misfortunes, they help increase the child's stress and the chance that misbehavior can become a full-blown crisis. It is important for adults to understand that a young person under stress and misbehaving needs to talk. Effective adults help young people in stress put language to their thoughts and feelings, which often makes it **unnecessary** for the child to act out his feelings through challenging behaviors.

Top Down, Bottom Up

For both young people and adults, our brains deal with information in two ways. Incoming sensory information, with the exception of smell, goes to a part of the brain called the thalamus which acts as a router sending that information to either the prefrontal cortex (the logical, thinking brain system) or the survival brain system (amygdala). If it goes to the logical brain system, the information can be processed logically and decisions made. If the information goes to the survival brain, the person reacts. So, based on where it is sent: you either think then react, or you react then think. This is called bottom-up processing (reacting then thinking) and top-down modulating (thinking then reacting). The more experiences people have handling tough situations, the more quickly and easily they will be able to access their logical brain system. Think about some of the young people you work with. If they lack experience thinking logically, the sensory information will go straight to the amygdala and they react. If this is the case (and this is the tough part for us), then we are punishing something they can't control. What do they need to make good decisions? They need to be able to access their prefrontal cortex quickly to modulate from the top of the brain. Instead, where are they operating? They are operating in their non-thinking, purely reactive survival system. As the experienced helpers, we need to avoid any of *our own* six factors: being in a bad mood; feeling helpless; the violation of personal values; feeling embarrassed or uncomfortable; personal triggers; and personal stress. We need to override our reactions and to access our logical system. Otherwise, we become counter-aggressive and get right into the fray with the young person!

The brain matures (decides which pathways it does and doesn't need – a process called apoptosis) and reorganizes based on our experiences. One important area of reorganization is in the prefrontal cortex, which handles abstract cognitive abilities as well as impulse control. In children, the brain has not yet matured to reorganize planning and impulse control so they have little impulse control. Adolescent brains are beginning to attain these higher-level skills of planning and impulse control. Adult brains are able to plan rather than just react and have control over their impulses. Again, this is assuming normal patterns of growth and development. Sometimes we expect behavioral responses that are not compatible with levels of brain maturation. The younger the person, the more assistance they will need from an adult to co-regulate to help them learn to self-regulate.

The Role of the Brain in Conflict and Counter-Aggression

The neuro-cognitive approach is contrary to old cognitive theory. Emotions are not feelings. Emotions are states (templates) that trigger behavior based on how the brain appraises the world around it. If it sees something scary, it reacts by designing an emotional template that tells the body to behave in a "scared" manner. The opposite is true with "happy" states. Once the emotional template has been designed and the body behaves in a certain way, the brain may think about what happened and assign it a label or feeling—scared or happy.

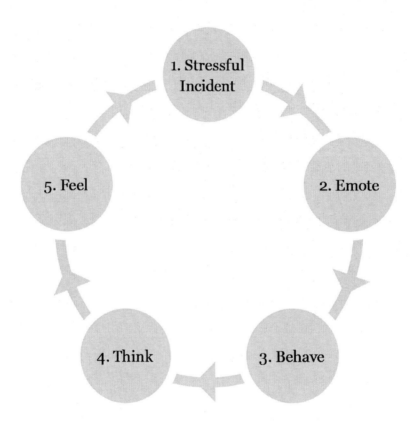

The Cycle of Neuro-Experience

- The process begins with a young person's irrational beliefs triggering a stressful event. Stress leads to beliefs/emotions that lead to behaviors that elicit the reactions of adults. If you are not trained to recognize these triggers and control them, you will mirror their behavior.
- Continued stress leads to more emotions that lead to additional behaviors that elicit more intense reactions of adults.
- Emotional overload leads to increasingly aggressive behavior that causes severe counter-aggression in adults that can ultimately lead to a full-blown crisis.

As the adults in the situation, we have the maturity to step back and not let our emotional reaction get the better of us. We need to do this for two reasons. Emotions are not a cognitive function; they do not help us to think about the best interests and needs of the young person in a specific moment. In addition, young people learn through imitation (mirror neurons) and we may not model acceptable behavior for them to learn from. Sometimes it is not easy to stop talking and emotionally step away, but that is the first step in our job as the adult in the room. Once we have stopped the cycle, we can then concentrate on helping the young person to begin to make the connection between their behavior, feelings, and the original stressful situation. We can also help the young person focus on managing stress and developing more appropriate coping skills.

Self-Reflection 12

Consider the following questions.

1) What are some of the factors that lead you to become counter-aggressive?

_____

_____

_____

_____

2) How do you cope with counter-aggressive feelings?

_____

_____

_____

_____

3) What strategies could you use to avoid turning a problem with a young person into a conflict if you were: in a bad mood; feeling helpless; feeling a violation of personal values; feeling embarrassed or uncomfortable; experiencing personal triggers; or experiencing personal stress?

_____

_____

_____

_____

The Brain and Pain or Punishment

Remember the old saying, "Sticks and stones may break your bones, but names can never hurt you?" Guess what? It's not true. Sticks and stones may break your bones, but names can and do hurt. According to converging evidence reported in a new review in *Current Directions in Psychological Science*, physical and social pain are processed in some of the same regions of the brain.

Physical pain has two components, sensory and emotional. The sensory part of physical pain is mapped in the brain depending on which part of the body is hurt. The emotional component (how distressing your brain determines the pain to be) is registered in the dorsal anterior cingulate cortex. That's also where the sting of social pain is processed.

Inflicting pain and punishing to "make them pay" just do not make good neurological sense. What makes humans different from all other species is the fact that we have a thinking, decision-making, problem-solving part of our brain located right at the front of our heads—our pre-frontal cortex. It can sift through our stored life experiences (memories) and help us make the best decision possible based on what we know. Like all other animal species, we also have a reactive, non-thinking part of our brain that we need for survival in life and death situations—our amygdala.

We want to utilize the brain's ability to think about conflict and make conscious decisions not to respond to a young person's challenging behavior in conflict-fueling ways. The strategies that follow can be used to avoid getting caught in the downward cycle into crisis and primitive responses during moments of stress.

Strategy Sheet 3: Strategies for Working towards Self-Regulation

A. **Be aware of body language and emotional demeanor**. The amygdala can actually read emotion. It has inbuilt programs to detect friendship or threat by reading: eye contact, facial expression, vocal tone, gestures, and body language/posture cues.

B. **Use the "Broken Record Strategy"** (Valentine, 1994). Stay with the goal behavior. Avoid the manipulation. This technique is used to get your request across, even in the face of resistance or evasiveness. The technique is not intended to foster long-term communication, but rather to make sure your requests are responded to clearly and for you to avoid being manipulated.

   1. Make your request as simply and clearly as possible: "I need you to… [state your request]."
   2. When presented with an argument, respond with: "I understand that you … [repeat their argument or statement about your character]. Regardless, I need you to… [repeat initial request]." Do not add qualifiers or emotionally loaded statements. Simply repeat the clear, concise request.
   3. Repeat as many times as needed.

Story: Ralph and the Skateboard—The Broken-Record Technique in Action

Ralph, an eighth-grade student has defied school rules and is using his skateboard in the parking lot in front of the school. The staff member on duty approaches Ralph:

Teacher: Ralph, the school rules state that skateboards are not to be used in the parking lot. I need you to pick up your skateboard and take it to the asphalt in the play area behind the school.

Ralph (arguing): This school sucks! That's a dumb rule. The concrete is better here.

Teacher: I understand that you think this school sucks and it is a dumb rule. Regardless, I need you to pick up your skateboard and take it to the asphalt in the play area behind the school.

Ralph (trying to get a reaction): What's with you? Are you a parrot?

Teacher: I understand that you think I am a parrot. Regardless, I need you to pick up your skateboard and take it to the asphalt in the play area behind the school.

Ralph (trying again to get a reaction): You suck! All you can do is parrot stupid rules.

Teacher: I understand that you think I suck and parrot stupid rules. Regardless, I need you to pick up your skateboard and take it to the asphalt in the play area behind the school.

Ralph (pulling out the big guns—this one always works): F*ck you, bitch! I'm not doing anything a parrot tells me.

Teacher: I understand that you think I am a bitch and a parrot. Regardless, I need you to pick up your skateboard and take it to the asphalt in the play area behind the school.

Ralph (giving it one more shot): There's no f*cking way I'm going to!

Teacher: I understand that you say there is no f*cking way you are going to. Regardless, I need you to pick up your skateboard and take it to the asphalt in the play area behind the school.

Ralph (going in for the kill—if this doesn't goad her nothing will): You are bat-sh*t crazy; you know that?

Teacher: I understand that you think I am bat-sh*t crazy. Regardless, I need you to pick up your skateboard and take it to the asphalt in the play area behind the school.

Ralph, shaking his head and muttering obscenities, picks up his skateboard and heads to the play area.

The goal here is to stay focused on what you want the young person to do. Yes, there are several issues that may need to be dealt with later, and they should be dealt with later. However, right now, you need a certain behavior to occur (skateboarding in the back where it is safe). Note that the teacher did not bite on any of Ralph's attempts to derail her and get her off on a tangent. She kept her language neutral, her tone of voice even and calm, and her body language in check (i.e., no hands on hips, waggling fingers, or rolling eyes). She didn't bother to try and support the reason for the rule or even react to personal comments; she focused on the desired behavior and didn't stop until it happened. The first time you do this, you may have to "go around the proverbial bush" quite a few times (and you may feel a bit silly being so rote, but rote helps you stay out of the manipulation zone). However, if you can be consistent, your reputation will quickly precede you. Your young people will know that arguing is futile because you simply won't let them manipulate you and that you won't get mad and off-track—which is what they want! Later in the day, or even the next day, when feelings aren't running high, you can talk to Ralph about inappropriate language, name calling and so on. That way, Ralph knows that he will not get away with any form of inappropriate behavior.

C. **Know your own tolerance level or "speed limit."** Everyone is different. Some people can take endless amounts of "guff" from young people before getting aggravated and some people can take very little. It doesn't matter what the worker across the hall is or is not willing to put up with. You are not that person. If we try and exceed our personal limits, we put ourselves in a position of becoming overly frustrated and more likely to lose our cool when put under stress. Young people learn very quickly that everyone has different expectations and often they will try to use this to their advantage. You hear things like, "Mr. So-and-So lets us." Just smile and say, "That's nice. However, I am not Mr. So-and-So," and carry on! Again, consistency is the key. If you give in even just once, you will be fighting the same battle for a long time.

D. **Be aware of your triggers**. Ask yourself this question: What does a young person do that makes me see red - that provokes that feeling that you are going to lose total control (that hands shaking, face flushed, heart racing angry feeling)? That is a trigger, and reacting to a trigger can pull you into a battle of wills very easily. We don't want to go there. The best way to avoid that battle is to be prepared. Have a plan in place ahead of time so that when your triggers are activated, you don't need to think about how to respond. You may need another person to take over for you, or you may just need to have something to do or say that forces you out of the cycle. Being forewarned is forearmed.

E. **Allow the young person (and yourself) time to cool off**. Both of you need to get out of your amygdala. Be sure to indicate that you will follow up later when they have calmed down and be sure to actually follow up. Remember, it can take 30 to 45 minutes for the stress hormones that trigger the fight-or-flight response to wash out of the body. Until that happens, it is easy for a situation to re-escalate.

F. **The "I Need to Go to Australia" technique**. Are you familiar with the children's book *Alexander and the Terrible Horrible No Good Very Bad Day*? In this story, Alexander has one of those days where everything that can go wrong does, and spectacularly! He gets so overwhelmed that he wants to run away to Australia. Young people can often use this as a "code" to let you know they are either getting overwhelmed, or are all the way there, and they need to step away and cool down. Set a specific location and time limit for this personal "time out" in an area where they will be supervised. After they have taken a few deep breaths and calmed themselves, they can return to the activity at hand.

G. **Be flexible. Apply the "So What?" test** (Townsend, 2000). Remember that fair does not necessarily mean equal. Revisit rules and expectations that serve only to impose control, as opposed to more meaningful rules that will influence quality of life. Simply stated, the "so what?" test could be applied to determine which expectations are more important. Ask yourself these questions:

So what if the young person is . . . . . . ?

What is the potential harm?

Or, so what if the child is doing . . . . instead of . . . . ?

This questioning allows you to examine the rule and infraction and decide if it is important enough to stop everything and deal with it.

Flexibility in rule enforcement from young person to young person can lead to an actual improvement of behavior for some.

H. **Teach the S.T.O.P. technique** (Shepard, 2015). **S**top what you are doing (talking, acting, etc.). **S**tate the problem, **T**alk about it, **O**wn your feelings, and **P**lan the next steps. Using a mnemonic like this helps young people take control of their own behavior and use adult assistance appropriately.

Memory

Simply stated, memory is about how our brain and body remember bits and pieces from our past so that these bits and pieces can be reactivated to our advantage in the future. There are various forms of memory that assist us in going through life, and memory is closely affiliated with the act of learning. In learning, one ideally takes a look at the specific facts of a situation and applies them in a way that is helpful. Memory works in a similar way. All learning is based on prior learning and all memory is based, to some degree, on prior memories. Nancy Andreasen (2005), chair of psychiatry at the University of Iowa, stated that each person is comprised of 46 chromosomes and approximately 30,000 genes that have somehow come together by the merger of a male and female parent. This merger results in the unique and individualized development of the actual person and his or her various parts (liver, heart, eye color, etc.). No one enters the world and remains exactly the same throughout life. The design of the brain must also be understood in this context. It develops from a combination of both the nature and nurture of the individual with memories resulting from multiple and complex cell connections based on genetics and experience.

The content of those memories becomes important as the person develops and grows. Through their daily interactions with others (how they respond to a simple question or task, for example), people display their experiential memories. Whether learning data or learning social cues, memory is critical in helping us to hold on to important information in the present that could be beneficial to us in the future. Without memory, we would be constantly experiencing "newness," which would prove to be detrimental to our existence. In essence, we would never learn from our successes or failures. We would just "be" in the moment.

Memory Systems: Explicit and Implicit Memory

Explicit Memory

Memories can be explicit or implicit. Explicit memories are memories that can be consciously recalled and verbalized easily. Explicit memories can be semantic (knowledge of data or facts in isolation and not connected to any particular event), such as a list of dates or capital cities that you need to memorize for a history test or the multiplication tables many of us memorized in elementary school. Explicit memories can also be episodic (personal life events connected to other people or events), such as your first kiss or where you were when the planes hit the World Trade Center. We use this type of memory to remember our daily schedule or what we did last summer.

Implicit Memory

Implicit memory is a type of memory in which early or previous experiences are encoded without conscious awareness. Implicit memories can be as simple as remembering how to do something without conscious awareness (like tying your shoes or riding a bike) or more complex social memories. These memories are not thought about consciously, but they are demonstrated in our attitudes and behaviors. A strong emotional reaction to someone you have never met before is an example of implicit memories in action (Cozolino, 2006).

We are born with immature brains and our first experiences with parents or caretakers become our earliest memories. These elements of sensations, perceptions, and images are implicit memories—memories that form the basis of our mental model of our environment. Continued experiences in life allow us to create generalized nonverbal conclusions about the world around us, and these conclusions guide our ongoing perceptions and actions (Badenoch, 2008).

While explicit memories are contextual to a time and place, implicit memories are not. When implicit memories are activated, we believe that they are there because of something happening in the present when in fact we are interpreting a present-day experience with the mental models we created in the past. For example, a whiff of cologne or a song causes you to feel a particular emotion, even though you are not thinking about the event associated with the emotion that the smell or song initially triggered. Implicit memories and the mental models they create can give us a perceptual bias, impacting behavior and how we approach certain situations. Because they are unconscious, we can be unaware that they are, in fact, driving our behavior and possibly making us look quite irrational in the eyes of those around us.

The Impact of Early Social Memories

There is a generally accepted belief that we have no memories before the age of two or three, but neuroscience is showing us that actually may not be true. Every experience that has any meaning to us, either positive or negative, is stored as a memory. It just may not be a memory we can access readily or put into words.

In Chapter 3, we talked about two limbic system structures, the amygdala and the hippocampus. In the case of early social memories, the amygdala processes and stores memories that are very emotionally laden, such as fear or terror. Remember the amygdala is fully mature at birth. Babies can feel intense emotions, but they are not able to understand them in any context. The hippocampus does not fully mature until approximately age three or four. This is the reason that we are unable to organize memories in terms of a sequence of events and therefore generally cannot remember things that occurred in that time period. It is not until the hippocampus is fully mature that we can begin to remember explicit memories, memories that we are concisely aware of and can tell a story about. We can, however, remember sensation and emotion from early years—just not the events surrounding those "body" memories. These remain as implicit memories.

If we experience extremely stressful or scary things, our brains protect us by producing chemicals that numb our physical pain, as well as interfere with the storage of these memories. Instead of storing them as explicit memories, which would be painful to remember, it stores them as implicit memories. These are often later expressed as an unconscious reaction to stressful situations and we have no idea why we are reacting like that.

Have you ever smelled a stranger's cologne as they walk by or heard a song on the radio and all of a sudden have a flood of memories (good or bad)? That happens because our brains have made a "good enough" match. The unconscious brain, as a way of keeping us safe, just needs a good enough match, as an exact match could take too long and put us at risk. Something or someone that simply reminds us of either a wonderful or a horrible memory from our past triggers an automatic response. If the trigger is negative, we will likely respond with fight or flight. In these cases, we feel great or awful, but we have no idea why because the memory is still implicit.

There are also times when our implicit memories can become explicit. If someone does something physical—raising a hand or reaching for a belt, for example—the implicit "body" memory can be (but are not always) pushed into our consciousness. These memories are called state-dependent memories. Even if this doesn't happen, early memories always show themselves in our behavior. We may not understand why we act in a specific way; our responses may not seem rational to others (and sometimes even to us); and they often cause problems down the road.

Trauma

In relational work, there are three commonly accepted levels of stress. First, the general stress state, or acute stress, which occurs typically in day-to-day events. The second is abuse or conflict, a more significant form of stress (chronic stress). This form of stress is intense and can cause us to reevaluate our circumstances. Finally, there is trauma. The *DSM IV* (American Psychiatric Association, 2000) defines trauma as "a direct personal experience of an event that involves actual or threatened death or serious injury, or other threat to one's physical integrity; or witnessing an event that involves death, injury, or a threat to the physical integrity of another person; or learning about unexpected or violent death, serious harm, or threat of death or injury experienced by a family member or other close associate. The person's response to the event must involve fear, helplessness, or horror (or in children the response must involve disorganized or agitated behavior)."

As a general rule, chronic abuse and trauma impede brain maturation and interfere with the normal bottom-up development and integration of the brain systems. Keep in mind that the brain is molded by experience. Every sight, sound, and thought leaves an imprint on specific neural circuits, modifying the way future sights, sounds, and thoughts will be perceived. All relationships, and especially primary relationships, impact the developing brain profoundly, for better or worse. When children feel safe and supported, their brains develop in a very coherent manner; but if they don't feel safe and connected in their primary relationships, their brains develop in a disrupted way.

Types of Trauma

Trauma is an experience that the brain processes and internalizes. There are several types.

Type 1: Single overwhelming event

Type 2: Repeated victimization

 A. Multiple traumas—resilient
 B. Multiple traumas—overwhelmed

Type 3: Extreme trauma—multiple experiences, typically beginning in early childhood.

Signs & Symptoms

Although traumatized adults are typically troubled by intrusive thoughts and images, children tend to re-experience trauma differently (Stien & Kendall, 2004; Putnam, 1997).

They can have:

Nightmares (Pynoos & Nader, 1988): Children experience terrifying dreams that replay the event with all the feelings of fear, terror, and helplessness that they experienced during the actual event.

Traumatic play (Terr, 1981): Children re-experience trauma through play that reenacts elements or themes of the event. It differs from regular play as it is monotonous and the same themes keep emerging—terror, helplessness, death, etc.

Behavioral reenactments (Terr, 1981): This is similar to traumatic play but in this case involves everyday activities. For example, a child who was abused would engage in sexually provocative behavior.

Psychophysiological reenactments (Terr, 1990): Under stress, a child may re-experience all the physical sensations that they experienced during the trauma.

In addition to these four ways of re-experiencing trauma, children experiencing a single, overwhelming event will have some or all of the following symptoms (Pynoos et al., 1997):

1. **Physical symptoms** (Terr, 1990), with no organic cause, e.g., headaches, stomach aches, rashes, shortness of breath.
2. **Anxiety** (Pynoos et al., 1997). They worry that the event will happen to them again in just the same way. Thus, they learn to avoid anything that dredges up thoughts of the initial trauma. Besides inducing fears from the event, trauma intensifies normal childhood fears.
3. **Depression or overwhelming sadness** (Pynoos et al., 1997).

4. **Hyperarousal/inability to concentrate** (Pynoos et al., 1997).
5. **Aggressive behavior/temper tantrums** (Pynoos et al., 1997).
6. **Irritability/unusual jumpiness** (Pynoos et al., 1997).
7. **Pessimism** (Terr, 1990).
8. **Dissociative behavior** (Putnam, Helmers, & Trickett, 1993). This can range from daydreaming and/or having an imaginary friend to voices with identities and functions and/or fragmented personality with identities and functions.

Children with complex or Type-2 trauma can also experience: problems regulating emotions and self-regulating; alterations in their conscious memory; a damaged self-concept and identity: cognitive impairment/rigid thinking; hyperactivity/attention problems; problems relating to others; feelings of little hope for the future; or feelings of rage and hatred (Stien & Kendall, 2004).

Diagnosing trauma requires evaluation by a trained mental-health professional. People working directly with young people have a major role in the identification and referral process. Awareness and understanding of trauma and its signs and symptoms is the first step towards trauma-informed practice.

Generational Trauma and Historic Distrust

Generational trauma is cumulative emotional and psychological wounding over the lifetime and across generations, emanating from massive group trauma. While generational trauma exists worldwide, the residential school experience of the Indigenous Peoples of Canada or the similar Aboriginal experience in Australia are examples of generational trauma. Social disruption and personal trauma is transferred across generations and can alter human genes. This can lead to historic distrust that can complicate helping and makes connection more difficult initially.

Trauma and the Brain

Trauma is powerful and creates experiences that are imprinted on the brain for a lifetime. One of the most significant forms of trauma occurs at the relational level. Abuse and extreme stress during childhood can impair early brain development and metabolic and immune system function, leading to chronic health problems, especially when the stress is inflicted by those in close relationship with the young person. This happens in part because child abuse leaves markers on a child's genes that can alter fundamental biological processes increasing the risk for a wide range of physical and psychiatric health conditions. These genetic markers also make the child more susceptible to developing post-traumatic stress disorder if they experience other types of trauma later in life. Experience becomes biology.

Childhood trauma interferes with normal brain development. Earlier in this chapter, we talked about how the amygdala and hippocampus are affected by trauma. In addition, when experiences are traumatic, the pathways getting the most use are those in response to the trauma; this reduces the formation of other pathways needed for adaptive behavior. The overdevelopment of certain pathways and the underdevelopment of others can lead to impairment later in life (Perry et al., 1995).

Brain development continues in the school-age years, but more slowly. During this stage, neural pathways are pruned or eliminated and myelinated to increase efficiency. This process allows young people to master more complex skills, including impulse control, emotional regulation, and focusing their attention. If this process is interrupted or interfered with, these abilities do not develop appropriately.

The impact of trauma also depends on the onset. If trauma continues into the school-age years from early childhood, the impact on overall functioning is greater. If it begins during the school-age years, it will have a different impact than trauma that begins in early childhood. Trauma occurring in later childhood (school-age) seems to result in more acting-out behaviors. Early childhood trauma appears to result in withdrawal, depression, and self-blame (Manly, 2001; Kaplow & Widom, 2007).

Trauma during adolescence, when a major period of neural pruning occurs, disrupts the development of the part of the brain that supports attention, concentration, reasoning, and advanced thinking. It also negatively affects how this part of the brain effectively communicates with other brain systems. This can lead to impulsive and risk-taking behaviors.

How Trauma Affects Learning

As we have just seen, trauma in childhood can affect concentration, memory, and organizational and language abilities. In turn, these can lead to problems with academic performance, inappropriate behavior in the classroom, and difficulty forming relationships.

Symptoms resulting from trauma can directly impact a student's ability to learn. Students may be distracted by intrusive thoughts about the trauma, which interfere with their ability to pay attention in class, to study, or to do well on tests. Exposure to violence can lead to decreased IQ and reading ability. Frustration from experiencing any of the above can lead to avoiding school or to quitting school altogether.

Traumatic experience can disrupt a young person's ability to relate to others and to successfully regulate their emotions. In the classroom, this can lead to unacceptable types of behavior, which can result in reduced time in the classroom, suspensions, and expulsions. Long-term results of exposure to trauma can lower overall grades and reduce the probability of graduation.

Working with Chaos, Stress, and Trauma

Distressed young people often suffer from lack of motivation as a result of feeling unempowered or overpowered by others. Many of these young people present behaviors that are off-putting and frustrating, making it tough for the people who work with them. It is important to remember that what might appear to be, on the surface, bad behavior or a bad attitude could also be symptomatic of living with chaos, stress, and/or trauma. But just because young people may be exhibiting these types of behaviors now doesn't mean it will always be that way. Neuroplasticity gives us hope for transformation.

Resiliency and Transformation

Resilience is defined as the ability to bounce back, to adapt properly to stress and adversity by flexibly applying necessary skills. We all have some level of resiliency and the more we learn, the more skills we attain; the more practice we get at making it through difficult situations, the more resiliency we have in general. Think of resiliency as a journey rather than a destination. Resiliency can ebb and flow depending on our life situation and the resources at our disposal.

Transformation occurs when a profound and radical change happens. We know that all interpersonal interactions affect the brain. We know that our brain's function determines how we perceive, think, and behave and our emotions also affect these things. Secure, non-threatening environments help us function at maximum cognitive efficiency. In abused young people, positive therapeutic relationships can interactively regulate negative states and thus help buffer the effects of traumatic stress. To help children affected by chaos, trauma, and stress transform, we must help to create an environment that enhances positive brain development and a safe environment in which to experience new relationships. New and better experiences can change the brain. It is never too late. We always have a window of hope and opportunity due to the plasticity of the brain.

Self-Reflection 13

Think about a person you consider resilient.

1) What characteristics or protective factors did they have that made them resilient?

_____

_____

_____

_____

2) How did they get that way?

_____

_____

_____

_____

3) Who was the critical person, or people, in their lives that affected their resilience, and how did they become resilient?

_____

_____

_____

_____

4) Do you think you are a resilient person? Why or why not?

_____

_____

_____

_____

Strategy Sheet 4: Strategies for Working with Chaos, Stress, and Trauma

A. **Create a safe and predictable environment** (Stien & Kendall, 2004). Safety and stability are basic needs for all people, but more so for young people coming from chaos, stress, or trauma, and particularly for those young people in care. They have to adjust to new routines and rituals. The structure of their days is different, and the people around them are unfamiliar and therefore scary. They may express their confusion and fear by acting out. They may even try "testing" you with bad behavior to see if you will stick around. Although young people recover from trauma through the creation of strong, positive relationships with adults, their previous experiences can make those kinds of connections very frightening for them. It is ironic that the very people these young people need the most are the ones that they are most likely to attack or verbally abuse them. Safe environments need to be both physically and psychologically safe. Change is particularly difficult for traumatized young people. If routines need to change, give as much warning as possible so that they have time to adjust.

B. **Set limits** (Cole et al., 2005). You need to set some limits. We all need to be held accountable for our behavior. Traumatized young people may need to learn that following rules will make a positive difference in their lives. Many children who grow up amid violence and abuse have learned that rules are arbitrary. It is essential that any behavior support planning emphasizes positive behavioral supports and is not overly rigid. Be consistent.

C. **Help young people regulate their emotions and behavior** (Stien & Kendall, 2004). When you notice that a young person is having a difficult time, start by asking yourself, "What's happening here?" rather than "What's wrong with this kid?" They may have been triggered and are in their survival system where they are reacting rather than thinking. Watch for physical manifestations like clenched fists, red face, a "deer-in-the-headlights" look, rapid breathing, or getting ready to or bursting into tears. Talking them through it helps them regain a sense of control and feel safe. Start with "I see you're having a problem with…" or "You seem to be getting a little irritated" and then offer some choices (with at least one they might want to try). Over time, they will see that not only do you understand but that you care, and they may be more willing to ask for help openly when they need it.

D. **Give the young person some sense of control** (Perry, 2014; Cole et al., 2005). When a traumatized child feels they do not have control of a situation, they will predictably get more agitated. If they are given some choice or some element of control in an activity or in an interaction with an adult, they will feel safer, more comfortable, and they will be able to feel, think, and act more appropriately.

E. **Crisis intervention training for all staff** (Zelechoski et al., 2013). Our young people can be hyper-vigilant and easily aroused emotionally because their amygdala is working overtime. It does not take much for some relatively harmless behavior to escalate quickly into a full-blown crisis situation. Restraint at this point is counterproductive unless, for safety reasons, there is absolutely no other choice. Training in crisis intervention will reduce the number of escalations and allow the staff to work more productively with young people when crises happen. This type of training also allows staff to turn crisis situations into positive learning experiences rather than negative or punitive ones.

F. **Functional behavioral assessments** (Cohen, Berliner, & Mannarino, 2010). A traumatized young person who has difficulty regulating emotions or behaviors might benefit from a functional behavioral assessment and a behavior intervention plan. Considerations should include traumatic triggers, the young person's understanding of authority, and their ability to follow rules. Frequently, other clinical issues need to be factored in, as well as any academic considerations.

Secondary Trauma: Compassion Fatigue

Caring for or working with young people who have been affected by trauma can be stressful and can trigger personal reactions (Figley, 1995). Our focus is often on the young person, helping them to manage their behavioral and emotional reactions, and it is easy to forget that our own emotions can also be impacted. Often, we end up feeling overwhelmed, exhausted, and frustrated by the reactions of the young person and we experience "compassion fatigue," a form of secondary traumatic stress disorder. It is vitally important that anyone working with traumatized young people monitors their personal reactions, emotions and needs, and seeks support. This is particularly important if the adults were involved in the trauma because unresolved traumatic issues can easily rise to the surface. Proper self-care improves both the quality of care for the young people and our personal professional capacity.

One Final Thought... It Isn't Always Trauma

The signs and symptoms of trauma are many and varied. And, as you have seen in the last several pages, trauma symptoms can look like many other behavior issues. Everyone experiences trauma differently based on their resilience, protective factors, and resources and supports. What may be traumatic to one person may not be to another. Without a definitive diagnosis, jumping to the conclusion that behavior is trauma related may be incorrect; that is a job best left to the doctors, psychologists, and psychiatrists. However, the strategies in this chapter represent best practices in learning that will benefit all young people. When incorporated into a consistent daily routine, they will have a powerful effect on distressed young people. Merely discovering that success in their program is a realistic possibility can have a huge impact. Many successful adults who were raised in troubled homes or were faced with early life trauma attribute their achievements later in life to the support of a caring adult who helped them cope with their stress and channel their energy productively.

Chapter 5

Growing Up—How the Brain Changes

....

Biology gives you a brain. Life turns it into a mind. Jeffery Eugenides

How the Brain Develops

Based on the way it is used in life, the human brain builds itself from the bottom up and from the back to the front. It develops from the least complex to the most complex areas. While significantly interconnected, each of the regions of the brain mediates distinct functions. At birth, the brainstem areas responsible for regulating cardiovascular and respiratory function must be intact for the infant to survive. This must be organized in utero.

Bottom to Top – Back to Front

After the brainstem, the midbrain develops. This area focuses on survival functions such as safety and threat response. Next in the developmental order is the limbic area, which deals primarily with our feelings and emotions. The largest and the last parts of the brain to develop are the frontal lobes and sections of the brain that provide the ability to reason, to plan, to anticipate, and to predict. These parts of the brain develop most rapidly during adolescence and early adulthood.

As the brain is developing from bottom to top, this process is influenced by a host of neurotransmitters, neurohormones, and neuromodulator signals. These signals help target cells to migrate, differentiate, and form connections. These crucial neural networks originate in the lower-brain areas and project to every other part of the developing brain. This allows these systems the unique capacity to communicate across multiple regions simultaneously and therefore to provide an organizing and orchestrating role during development later in life.

Right then Left

The right hemisphere develops first and grows quite rapidly during the first 18 months of life. This coincides with the development of sensory and motor capabilities that go hand in hand, matching our relational and ecological experiences. At the same time, the basic structures of attachment and emotional regulation are being established in the right side of the frontal lobe, while development of the left hemisphere is slowed (Schore, 1994). During the second year of life, the left hemisphere has a growth spurt as babies learn to move about their world. The focus of the frontal lobes shifts to the learning of language and eye–hand coordination. The corpus callosum, the bundle of neural fibers that connect the hemispheres, begins to develop near the end of the first year. This allows for the integration of the hemispheres' capabilities, although alternating growth spurts occur generally in the hemispheres until the age of 12.

The brain encodes our early years experiences. With enough repetitions it becomes a mental model. These models allow us to create generalized expectations of whether relationships are trustworthy or not. As we mature, they stay below the level of consciousness (implicit because of the age at which they were formed), constantly influencing our perceptions.

Many of our young people can appear difficult to work with because they have grown up with negative experiences (neglect, abuse, trauma). They are leery of adults and anticipate bad things at every turn. This becomes a self-fulfilling prophecy as their perceptions often cut off access to empathetic and caring others. Understanding how the brain does this potentially helps us to change the mental models to ones that provide internalized support for better self-regulation and behavior.

The Development of the Executive Function

Executive function is a term that describes a set of cognitive abilities that control and regulate other abilities and behaviors. Executive functions are necessary for appropriate, conscious control of our behavior. They help us with: time-management; shifting focus; attention; planning; organizing; and problem-solving. There are three main categories of executive function: *self-regulation*—the ability to control impulses and to focus and filter out distractions around us; *cognitive flexibility*—the ability to think about new things, plan for the future, and solve problems; and *working memory*—the ability to hold and manipulate several things in our mind simultaneously (Miyake et al., 2000).

We are not born with these abilities. They develop with time and practice and are affected by both our genes and our experiences. The main part of the brain involved in executive function is the frontal lobe, specifically the prefrontal cortex. This is the last part of the brain to fully mature and develop, usually in the early-to-mid 20s. The prefrontal cortex, with its enhanced thinking and reasoning capabilities, is one reason for the big difference between the ways adults and young people react. Adults process emotions through pathways in the prefrontal cortex where the brain is able to look at its own processes, giving adults more cognitive input about their feelings. This, in turn, helps to control emotional outbursts. The adult's response to frustration is generally more reasoned than that of a young person.

Below, you will see a chart exploring the normal development of the executive functions over time. It is important to note that all these stages are approximate and are indicative of average human development. Life situations and experiences can speed up or slow down this process.

Function	Stages				
	Infants (0-2)	**Early Childhood (3-5)**	**School Age (6-12)**	**Adolescents (13-18)**	**Adults (18-25)**
Self-Regulation	Voluntary passive control of arousal evident around 3 months; during 2nd year moves to more active methods of self-control (Bell & Calkins, 2012).	Able to delay acting on needs/ wants by 4 years old (Garon et al., 2008).	Rapid development. Able to ignore irrelevant visual stimuli and information by 7 years old (Garon et al., 2008).	Able to focus attention on or ignore information as required and can move back and forth between the two (Blakemore & Choudhury, 2006).	Self-control should be stable and consistent (Dawson et al., 2012).
Cognitive Flexibility	Able to figure out how to find a recently hidden object by 9-11 months (Diamond, 1990 a, b).	Understand and apply different rules in different situations 2-5 years old (Isquith, Gioia, & Espy, 2004).	Begin to develop flexible thinking at 7-9 years old. Begin to adapt behavior to multiple changing situations at 10-12 years old (Zelazo et al., 2003).	Improved ability to shift focus. Improved ability to adapt behavior in changing situations (Blakemore & Choudhury, 2006).	Cognitive skills well developed. Capable of solving complex problems (Dawson et al., 2012).
Working Memory	Develop object permanence— can remember something after it is gone (Bertenthal et al., 2013).	Can recall a sequence of events and differentiate between 2 categories (Diamond, 1990 a, b).	Develop more complex memory. Begin to understand memory and use strategies to recall things (Diamond, 1990 a, b).	Memory continues to improve. Development of metamemory— understand memory and how it works (Blakemore & Choudhury, 2006).	Can remember multiple things and how they interact or impact each other (Conklin et al., 2007).

Typical Executive Function Development

Effective executive functioning first identifies that there is a problem to be solved by attending to external and internal environmental cues. It also uses information provided by working memory to assess the possible solutions to the problem and to come up with a plan of action. Poor executive functioning is not necessarily related to intelligence (Friedman et al., 2006). Highly intelligent people can have significant problems with decision-making, planning, and social situations. Optimal executive functioning relies on an integration of various parts of the brain and signals that can go back and forth quickly and easily. When we have good integration, we are better able to control our social and emotional behavior.

Controlling and Regulating Attention

As we mentioned before, our ability to control our actions is not innate. It emerges as we develop and is necessary for positive social relations and successful learning. Emotional self-control appears to play a role in child resiliency and later adjustment. Children who do not learn self-control in preschool can develop aggressive habits of interaction that create problems for the adults around them. In addition to decision-making, problem-solving, and predicting, the brain's frontal lobe plays a large role in monitoring the limbic area in an effort to keep emotions under control. The part of the frontal lobe that appears to be closely involved in monitoring emotions is called the anterior cingulate (AC). The AC becomes highly activated whenever someone attempts to resolve conflicting ideas or when they face distress. When disagreements arise that can't seem to be resolved, the brain feels distress and this prompts the amygdala to generate negative emotions, which can escalate unless some mechanism intervenes to provide restraint. In these situations, it is the job of the AC to rein in the amygdala, allowing us to temper the expression of distress and resolve conflict in a civil manner.

The Adolescent Brain

In adults, various parts of the brain work together to evaluate choices, make decisions, and act accordingly. A young person's brain doesn't appear to work this way. One reason is that the prefrontal cortex is always a work in progress. The primary part of the logical brain that helps adults make good decisions is immature and underdeveloped in teenagers (Blakemore & Choudhury, 2005). In fact, it may not fully develop and mature until the mid-20s or later. In addition, teenagers experience a wealth of growth in synapses during adolescence. Just as in the earlier remodeling periods, following the boom of growth the brain starts pruning away the synapses that it doesn't need so that the remaining ones are more efficient in communicating. In humans, this maturation process starts in the back of the brain and moves forward, so that the prefrontal cortex, that vital center of control, is the last to be pruned and mature.

Metacognition

Thus, because the pre-frontal cortex is often not fully developed, teenagers are not using the part of their brains that plays an essential role in impulse control, decision-making, planning, and prediction. Adult brains are also better wired to notice errors in decision-making and pick up on them more quickly. This comes from a more mature frontal lobe that is used more extensively. It also comes from an ability that comes with brain maturity—metacognition. Metacognition is the ability to think about your thinking. It is a process that requires self-monitoring, self-representation, and self-regulation processes, which are regarded as integral components of the mature human mind. These capacities are used to regulate one's own thinking and to maximize one's potential to think. This ability comes after that massive neural pruning that comes in adolescence. While it may sound counterintuitive, synaptic connections and neurons that have not been used enough waste a great deal of blood, oxygen, and energy. Pruning them out keeps the brain focused and efficient (Doidge, 2007).

Apoptosis

Until that pruning and rewiring are complete, teenagers and young adults tend to perform cognitive tasks (make decisions, problem solve, and predict the future) largely in their temporal lobes. The shift to the frontal lobes does not happen until later in life, regardless of level of education (Springer, McIntosh, Wincour, & Grady, 2005). This processing shift within the brain is another example of plasticity. Often, we ask young people to elicit their metacognitive awareness before they have acquired maturity and proficiency in this area; in essence, we ask them to do something they are not yet capable of developmentally.

The frontal lobes, or what Daniel Goleman (1998) calls the "just say no" section of the brain, may not be fully mature and functional until the early-to-mid-20s. But one area of the teenager's brain that is fairly well developed early on is the nucleus accumbens, the part of the brain that seeks pleasure and reward. Studies using imaging techniques have compared brain activity when receiving a small, medium, or large reward. Teenagers exhibited exaggerated responses to medium and large rewards compared to children and adults. The teenagers' brains showed minimal activity when presented with a small reward in comparison to the brains of adults and children (Powell, 2006).

Young people (with immature decision-making capabilities and a strong desire for reward) can appear to display rebellious, risk-taking behavior and an increase in potential addiction issues. However, all the news is not bad. During this time, the brain is acting like a sponge; it can soak up new information and change to make room for it. The increased growth and neural pruning increase plasticity, and plasticity can help young people to pick up new skills and to build new neural pathways through better and positive experiences. This is an opportune time for those of us working with young people to re-sculpt their experiences.

Self-Reflection 14

We know that adolescent brains differ from adult brains.

1) What implications does the information about the development of the teenage brain have for reconsidering rules and responsibilities for this age group?

_____

_____

_____

_____

2) Think about how your program handles rules and responsibilities for adolescents. Knowing what you know now, are there things that might be changed? When might they not be changed?

_____

_____

_____

_____

3) What implications might this information have for zero tolerance-type policies or mindsets?

_____

_____

_____

_____

When the Brain and Body Development are Not in Sync

Adolescence is the period of development between childhood and adulthood. When we are very young children, parents are responsible for regulating our behavior. Once we become adults, we become responsible for our own behavior (Casey & Jones, 2010). During adolescence, the shift from parental responsibility begins and this is often a difficult time for people living with or working with this age group. We mentioned earlier that adolescents engage in more risk-taking behaviors; they experiment more, and they can be impulsive. There is also a shift of influence during this time as teenagers become more involved with their friends and less involved with their family. Adolescents struggle to figure out "who they are" as they work towards becoming independent.

The "X" Factor and the Existential Crisis of Becoming an Adult

Mary Wood (2007), Professor of Special Education at the University of Georgia, calls the developmental shift in perceived authority and responsibility of adults, an existential (relating to life or existence) crisis. Wood believes there are three stages of development in the gradual shift in the source of authority and responsibility from adults (external control) to themselves (internal controls): the *pre-existential*, *existential*, and *post-existential* phases.

1. **Pre-existential**: preschool-age children (typically ends before age 8). Children in this phase believe that adults have absolute power and control. The tattling that is seen at this stage is a form of deference to the perceived authority of the adults around them. Children at this stage do not see themselves as having any role in problem-solving. It is solely the job of the adults.
2. **Existential**: early elementary school age children (typically ends between ages 9 & 12). The shift in responsibility and authority begins in this phase. These young people become more and more self-reliant, initially seeing themselves as independent but not "responsible." As they realize that adults can't solve all their problems, they begin to also accept the need to be responsible. The existential crisis occurs at this point and can be a dilemma. Do they act independently or do they rely on adult intervention? What do they do when adults don't do a very good job of handling a situation in their minds (divorce, death, family violence, etc.)? In this phase, many young people are extremely anxious and insecure and their behavior "mirrors" these feelings. They test adults, they try to control them, and when the skills they have to help themselves through tough situations fail, they act out. Even when they have the skills they need, not having adults to help them through a rough patch can cause a failure of resolution of their existential crisis. After several experiences like this, these young people struggle with authority on a regular basis. If this phase is not adequately resolved, these young people become manipulative and controlling. They will question you at every turn and doubt themselves at the same time. They have no trust in adults in general and they will resist authority at all costs. They may want approval, but they do not want your guidance.
3. **Post-existential**: upper-elementary- and secondary-school-age young people (typically begins about age 10 but will vary based on life experiences). When this stage is reached, the crisis

has been resolved. They may still look to adults for direction if they respect their authority, but they have the self-control and problem-solving skills to take responsibility for their own behavior. They may not have all the skills they need to be successful and productive in society yet, but they are moving forward and learning to be independent and to behave responsibly. Adults working with young people in this phase are more of a "guide on the side" than a "sage on the stage." Essentially, they serve as role models, encouraging independence, appropriate problem-solving strategies and forward planning.

Wood believes that it is vital that those of us who work with troubled young people are not only aware of the developmental process, but we are also aware of where each young person is on that existential continuum. If we ignore this and respond to them only chronologically instead of developmentally, we do it at our own peril. Knowing where a young person is existentially gives us a great deal of information about how they perceive authority and how much personal responsibility they are willing to take. This is where the "X" factor comes in. The "X" factor is "the changing paradigm for guiding [young people] through this developmental process" (Wood et al., 2007, p. 106). If most of the young people you work with are in the existential crisis stage regardless of age or size, you need to respond to them with strategies that are effective at this stage. If you hear yourself saying things like "They are old enough to know better" and you feel their behavior has just proved that they aren't, then you need to reconsider how you respond. Remember, self-regulatory skills are not innate. We are not born with them. We learn them in our environments. But if for some reason, we haven't acquired self-regulation, we need to have these skills modeled for us and taught to us, regardless of the chronological age of the child.

Instead of jumping to the conclusion that something is "seriously wrong" with a young person when they act out, Wood (2007) suggests you consider the following:

Is the behavior defensive? Are they trying to protect themselves from stress and anxiety?

Look beyond the behavior. What feelings or anxieties might be driving this behavior and what defense mechanisms are they using? (Refer back to Chapter 3.)

How effective are these mechanisms?

What other behavior(s) could be taught for better results?

Strategy Sheet 5: Growing a Grown-Up Brain

A. **Start where the young person is developmentally and go from there**. If a young person is in the pre-existential phase, Wood (2007) suggests they need an adult to help them learn how to behave appropriately. They need your protection and they are relying on you as the authority figure. You should direct their behavior, handle their problems, and teach them how to meet others' expectations. At this stage, you need to be a caring expert. If they are in the existential crisis phase, you need to maintain authority and control through structure and routine. Think of yourself more as a benign dictator and less like Attila the Hun. You need to enforce rules of conduct gently and use consequences when the conduct is inappropriate, but you need to have logical consequences from reasonable rules. Power for the sake of power might get you the behavior you want, but it will not get you developmental growth. You can encourage better choices and self-regulation and control through lots and lots of positive feedback and appropriate praise. Look for the good even amidst the bad. The more you talk about the good things, the more insight a young person will have about their behavior and others' behavior. In the pre-existential stage, you are essentially regulating their behavior for them. In this stage, you are co-regulating. Co-regulation is a parallel process. In many cases, troubled young people have not had sufficient logical experiences to provide them with the necessary reasoning and predicting skills that might be needed to make wise decisions. This is true even with typical children and adolescent young people. Healthy adults trained to recognize needs of young people must often step in to help them develop appropriate plans of action or ways of behaving. The co-regulator provides temporary assistance and steps away as soon as possible. In the post-existential phase, you want to guide growth while promoting independence. At this point the young person is self-regulating. Give enough direction for young people to be successful and use your behavior as a role model for problem-solving. Positive affirmations, evaluative feedback, group planning, and lots of discussions of options and what is and isn't appropriate help these young people on the road to true independence.

B. **Manage the extremes of behavior and emotion**. Pick your battles. Sometimes you do have to intervene—but not always. If behaviors are a threat to safety or health, damage of property, or they infringe on the human rights of others, then intervene; if not, ask yourself if it can be ignored. Behaviors that are irritating (and we really wish they would not be displayed but are not causing any of the above) can often be ignored. If you really would prefer it to stop, you can ignore and redirect. Interrupt while ignoring the behavior and give them something else to do that is more appropriate. This is not the time to talk about the behavior. Save that for later. If they transition as requested, it gives you an opportunity to affirm their good choice.

C. **Reduce power struggles**. Decide which rules are negotiable and which are non-negotiable. Determine your consequences and follow through. After you have done this, be sure they understand and are aware of the consequences of compliant and non-compliant behavior. It will reduce arguments. Don't threaten unless you are willing to follow through with your threat. They love to test you on this one! Avoid emotional responses (anger, sarcasm), bribing, or put-downs. Give simple directions with choices if appropriate. Walk away from the situation if you are feeling like you are losing control or the discussion is no longer effective. You can do this physically or, if that is not possible, do it verbally. Stop responding and do not allow yourself to be drawn back in. Calmly say, "This is not a good time to discuss this. We can talk about it later." And stick to it.

D. **Make your interventions calm and gentle**. Create an atmosphere of respect and model it in your language and behavior. Actively listen to the young person's point of view and validate their feelings. Use a calm voice and speak normally or even slightly slower. Be conscious of your facial expressions, body language, tone of voice, and gestures. If you must intervene, remove the student or remove the audience. Humor can be an effective tool as long as it is appropriate and does not make the young person the target. If the young person responds in a neutral or positive way during this time, you can be positive and engaging, offering encouraging feedback and instruction. If they respond in a negative manner, be business-like, following through on pre-determined consequences.

Not all bad behavior is indicative of an underlying pathology. Sometimes bad behavior is just a demonstration of the lack of a "skill set" to handle stress and anxiety in a more appropriate way. Of course, we want all young people to take responsibility for their behavior but, in many cases, we need to become part of the process and co-regulate. It is unreasonable for us to expect appropriate behavior from our young people if they don't know what they don't know. Self-regulation needs to be taught; the closer your management strategies are to the developmental level of the young person, the more receptive they will be to moving towards appropriate behavior and personal accountability.

Story: Jasper and the "Temper Tantrum"

Jasper was 16 and very big for his age. He looked closer to 20 and he used it to his advantage at every bar in town. Jasper was enrolled in a day program for young people with addictions after overdosing twice at "pharm parties." The young people in the program spent part of their day with their teacher and in groups, part of the day doing academic catch-up, and blocks of time doing work experience. Jasper had just washed out of a work placement in a restaurant/local hotspot bar that he had been really excited about. This wasn't the first time this had happened. He arrived at the program the next morning, sat down at a desk in the academic area, and put his head down. The day got started and Jasper remained sitting there, head in his hands. A staff member walked over to where Jasper was sitting, knelt down beside the desk, and quietly asked if there was anything that he needed. Jasper stood up, taking the desk with him. As the staff member wisely got out of the way, he pulled the desk off his body, threw it to the floor, cussing and swearing with every expletive he knew. He grabbed his binder and tore it to shreds, throwing bits and pieces of it around the room. He kicked another desk and he kicked the door. The swearing and yelling continued. No one moved. No one said a thing. After the initial explosion, the staff member walked to the back of the room and talked with another young person, keeping one eye on the situation. Jasper stomped around the front of the room, kicking any inanimate object he could reach. After several minutes of this, he ran out of steam, opened the door to the hallway, turned, and screamed, "I hate all of you! F&ck you!" He slammed the door and left the building. A call to his parents found Jasper at home, still emotionally upset but physically calm. When Jasper came in the next day to see his teacher, he informed her that he had lost his job placement because, as he put it, "he lost his sh*t with his stupid dumbass of a boss." When he was asked to do something that he thought was not his job, he initially politely refused but then really lost it when his supervisor pushed back. He ripped off his apron, threw his bill book and tray across the kitchen, swore, and walked out.

Activity 1: Jasper and the "Temper Tantrum"

You are Jasper's teacher/youth worker. He is sitting in your office and is really upset that he has lost another work experience placement. He wants you to help him get another job placement with a "better boss" because it wouldn't have happened if the boss hadn't been such a jerk.

Using the information from the story above:

1) Based on his age, what developmental level should Jasper be at according to Mary Wood?

_____

_____

2) What level do you think he is actually at? What details helped you make that decision?

_____

_____

3) With the brief bit of information that you have, do you see a pattern in Jasper's behavior?

_____

_____

4) Based on his age and size, how could Jasper's behavior lead to misunderstandings? What are some of the potential consequences of Jasper's behavior if he is not taught better self-regulation?

_____

_____

5) What strategy did the staff member use with Jasper? Would you have done something different? If so, what would you have done and why?

_____

_____

6) Think back to the reimbursements in Chapter 1. What might Jasper need?

_____

_____

7) Create a list of possible suggestions for how you could begin to help Jasper.

_____

_____

Chapter 6

The Power of the Moment

....

I've learned that people will forget what you said, people will forget what you did, but people will never forget how you made them feel. Maya Angelou

Young people experience conflict and crisis at some point in their lives. These experiences usually bring out strong emotions and often leave them feeling upset, bothered, and/or hurt. Understanding the often-complicated psychodynamics that are involved in these moments helps adults to better negotiate them by identifying the most effective ways to resolve these situations.

Conflict Management versus Crisis Support

Conflict is defined as a "strong disagreement between people, groups, etc., that results in often angry argument" (Merriam-Webster's online dictionary, n.d.). People in conflict generally experience some level of threat to their interests or needs. Conflict is beyond a simple disagreement. By the time a disagreement has reached the stage of conflict, the perceived misunderstanding and subsequently the threat, has become exaggerated. Whether or not the threat is real or perceived, the feelings of threat are real and the people involved will respond based on those feelings. Those feelings of threat often lead to the perception of limited options for resolution of the problem when there may, in fact, be multiple possibilities that exist. Conflict is a normal part of life and it occurs because we all have different needs and wants.

While conflict may be normal, how young people handle it can "make it or break it." Learning how to deal with conflict effectively, rather than avoiding it or making it worse, is crucial. When conflict is mismanaged, it can easily escalate into a crisis—"a difficult or dangerous situation that needs serious attention" (Merriam-Webster's online dictionary, n.d.). Earlier, we explained the need to teach self-regulatory skills; managing conflict is one of those skills. Many of the young people we see every day need our help and co-regulation to learn how to manage conflict in positive ways and to prevent it from escalating into a crisis.

The goal in conflict resolution is to build mutually beneficial relationships so that the parties involved can find a solution that meets the needs of everyone. In any conflict, there are three possible outcomes:

- Lose/lose
- Win/lose
- Win/win

In lose/lose nobody gets what they want and there is no resolution. Both parties are unhappy and resentment is likely to build in both parties until the problem is dealt with. In win/lose, one party gets what they want but the other doesn't. The winner is happy. The loser is not. A win/win outcome is the preferable outcome. In this case, both parties are satisfied with the resolution and no one "loses face." Many times when working with young people we end up "winning the battle but losing the war" when we resort to coercion to get the behavior we want. We stop the conflict but oftentimes we damage the relationship with that young person. Instead of reducing conflict down the road, we actually make the young person more willing to take us on. Before we can help young people learn to deal with conflict better, we need to understand how we, intentionally or not, can become part of the problem, creating what Nick Long (1965) calls "the conflict cycle."

Self-Reflection 15

Think back to a conflict or heated argument that you have had with a young person. Think about the sequence of events that occurred.

1) What and who started it? Was the initiating factor something that was said or something that was done?

_____

_____

_____

2) How did the person receiving that initial factor respond or react?

_____

_____

_____

3) What happened next? Continue until you have described the situation completely.

_____

_____

_____

_____

_____

4) How did it end? Who "won" the dispute in the short term? Who won in the long term?

_____

_____

_____

5) Did either party get what they wanted?

_____

_____

_____

6) If a "show of force" was used, did it stop further conflict with that person down the road?

_____

_____

_____

The Conflict Cycle

The conflict cycle model helps us to understand how a [young person] in stress creates feelings comparable to his or her own in adults, and if the adult is not trained, how the adult may mirror the [young person's] behavior" (Long, Wood, & Fecser, 2001). In Chapter 2, we talked about how experiences shape perception and drive behavior. In the conflict cycle:

1) A young person's negative self-concept or irrational beliefs are triggered by a stressful incident or event.
2) This event triggers these "irrational" thoughts and feelings in the young person.
3) Irrational feelings result in observable negative behaviors.
4) Adults observe this behavior and react to it, often in equally negative and counter-aggressive ways. This creates more stress, reinforces the young person's negative beliefs and fuels the next cycle (Long, 2014).

Conflict cycles often start with a small incident that escalates due to the alternating reactions and behaviors of the parties involved creating a looping or cyclical effect. These repeated loops or cycles build on each other rapidly and may result in emotional flooding, outbursts, or violence. What started out as a conflict can rapidly become a crisis.

Most of us consider ourselves to be rational and in control of ourselves and our emotions and yet we can all remember times when we allowed ourselves to get pulled into a conflict cycle with a young person. Unless adults can control their reactions to inappropriate behavior and have an awareness of their emotional buttons, we will escalate the incident and make it worse. Responding in a counter-aggressive manner is like trying to put out a small fire by throwing gasoline on it (Long, 2014). We know that much of the bad behavior we see is the way our young people have learned to express their feelings based on their life experiences. We know that if they have not learned appropriate coping and self-regulatory skills, we need to help them learn these skills, in part by modeling appropriate behavior. And yet we respond and react just as badly as they do. So why do we do it?

It is not unusual for an aggressive young person to cause the adult dealing with them to react counter-aggressively. Neurologically we mirror both the emotions and the actions of the aggressor. Once we respond in a counter-aggressive way, it often becomes a self-defeating power struggle. Even if we had no intention of getting into the fray, once we are in, it is very hard to stop. In addition, as rational and caring adults, it is very difficult to accept that we actually made it worse. Instead, our emotions flood and we feel righteous indignation. We use this to justify our bad behavior.

After analyzing more than 600 conflict cycles, Long (2014) found three main reasons why adults become counter-aggressive:

1) **Rigid and/or unrealistic expectations of behavior.** When in terms of behavior an adult's expectations differ from what they see, many believe that the young person has a problem

that needs to be fixed. Many adults believe that since they are the authority figure, young people **must** be obedient and respectful regardless of how the adult treats them. There is an expectation that young people will always be attentive and well behaved regardless of what is happening in their lives.

2) **Bad mood/bad day.** While adults have the unrealistic expectation that young people will behave well regardless of life stressors, the same adults become less tolerant of behavior infractions when they themselves are dealing with personal or professional stress. Under normal circumstances, they would be caring and supportive but when stressed, they can overreact and allow a conflict to become a crisis.

3) **Prejudging a troubled young person.** Young people whose reputations precede them are often the subject of behavioral assumptions on the part of adults. While we may give the benefit of the doubt to relatively well-behaved young people, we automatically assume the worst and often target those with a reputation. If we jump to conclusions about someone before we ascertain the facts, we can make assumptions that lead to conflict and crisis.

Insight into why troubled young people behave the way they do, and how their behavior can trigger emotional flooding and counter-aggressive reactions, stops adults from engaging and escalating an already stressful situation. Adults can acknowledge their counter-aggressive feelings and choose not to become ensnared in a power struggle. The focus then moves away from the behavior itself to the reason for the behavior. Instead of becoming a crisis where the result is lose/lose and relationships are often damaged, conflict can become an opportunity for new learning.

Let's revisit Jasper from Chapter 5 and examine a different adult response. Suppose the adult in that situation had allowed her counter-aggressive feelings to escalate the cycle.

Story: Jasper and the "Temper Tantrum" Part 2

Jasper was 16 and very big for his age. He looked closer to 20 and he used it to his advantage at every bar in town. Jasper was enrolled in a day program for young people with addictions after twice overdosing at "pharm parties." The young people in the program spent part of their day with their teachers and in groups, part of the day doing academic catch-up, and blocks of time doing work experience. Jasper had just washed out of a work placement in a restaurant/local hotspot bar that he had been really excited about. This wasn't the first time this had happened. He arrived at the program the next morning, sat down at a desk in the academic area, and put his head down. The day got started and Jasper remained sitting there, head in his hands. A staff member noticed that Jasper, as usual, was not doing what was expected. She walked over to where Jasper was sitting and tapped him on the shoulder and told him to "sit up and get to work." Jasper muttered, "Give me a break. Life sucks." In a slightly louder voice, the staff member told Jasper that he was not going to speak to her in that manner. Jasper lifted his head and said, "I'll speak to you any damn way I want, bitch." The staff member responded loudly "That's it! Go to the office. You'll be suspended for language." Jasper stood up, taking the desk with him. He pulled the desk off his body and threw it at the staff member, cussing and swearing with every expletive he knew. He grabbed his binder and tore it to shreds, throwing bits and pieces of it around the room. He kicked another desk, opened the door to the hallway, turned and screamed "F&ck you! I'll get you!" and headed for the hall. The staff member went after him, yelling that he was finished with this program. Nobody threatened her! Jasper lost it completely, turned around, and lunged towards her. It took several other staff members to pull him away and hold him until the police arrived. Jasper was suspended for six weeks pending psychiatric evaluation.

Activity 2: Jasper and the "Temper Tantrum" Part 2

1. Using the conflict cycle model, consider the following: What action brought out the first negative response? How did the other person react? How then did the first party respond? Complete the cycle this way.

2. Think about the brain's role in counter-aggression. What part of the brain (survival or logical) was each person likely in? What details led you to that conclusion? Did the brain part change or stay the same as the events unfolded? Explain what likely caused those changes.

3. During the series of stressful events, what do you think each person was thinking and/or feeling? What was their perspective of the whole situation? Describe the behaviors or conflict-fuelling responses that came from those feelings.

4. How did the staff member's reaction to the response of the student impact what happened next?

5. If we could rewind the cycle back to the point where Jasper muttered "Give me a break. Life sucks," what would have been a better response? Think about what Jasper needed at that point.

Strategy Sheet 6: Clear Communication

When we want a specific behavior to either stop or start we need to communicate clearly what it is we want. To avoid escalation, it is vitally important to use precise language to "say what we mean and mean what we say." Focus on what you want. For example, "Stop hitting" would be the use of start/stop directions. Use directions versus questions. For example, "Please start working on your assignment" versus "Can you start working?"

Sometimes, when young people behave inappropriately, we say things that actually encourage them to keep right on doing what they are doing. Below is a list of some types of unclear communications, an example, and the implied meaning of the example.

Type of Communication	Example	What You Are Actually Saying
A. **Encouraging Bad Behavior**	Do that again and see what happens.	Feel free to continue doing exactly what you are doing.
B. **Attempts to Change**	If you would just try a little harder.	You just want them to try—you don't actually want any real change. As Yoda said: "Do or do not. There is no try."
C. **Vague or Meaningless Directions**	Be mature. Use common sense.	If you don't have the qualities I'm talking about, it's okay to continue misbehaving.
D. **Unrelated Questions**	How many times do I have to tell you…? Did you not hear what I just said?	They can continue to act out as long as they have the answer to the question.
E. **Punishment**	Stop that or I'll send you to the office.	It's okay to keep misbehaving as long as they are willing to take the punishment.
F. **Stating the Obvious**	I can see that you didn't listen to me yesterday; or, I can see you came without your supplies again.	You are telling them something they already know. You aren't asking for anything specific. Be ready for the answer "No sh*t, Sherlock!
G. **Prophecy and Prediction**	You will end up in jail; or, You will never amount to anything.	Keep doing what you are doing since the outcome is already decided.
H. **Then Statements**	If you do that one more time, then you'll get…	They have a choice and either alternative is okay with you.
I. **Wishes and Shoulds**	I wish you would stop; or, You should know better.	You are stating a preference. They can ignore it if they chose.

Finally, avoid sarcasm. Sarcasm is often intended humorously, as a joke, and though sometimes it is funny, sarcasm generally relies on putting a young person down. The goal is to build up the relationship not damage it by making young people feel bad about themselves. Remember: "We get what we give."

Momentary Management

Momentary management is "in the moment" short-term support to get a young person back on track, preventing a problem from escalating. Once the situation is under control, it is critical to assess if the behavior is pervasive. If it is, it would be appropriate to access more intensive therapy.

Just like Jasper, young people often find themselves in situations that require an adult to either assist with logical processing for a specific moment or to help them think through a situation and their behavioral responses, acting as a co-regulator. Remember that most troubled young people have not had the appropriate opportunities to develop and practice the necessary reasoning and predicting skills. They do not always either make the best choices or respond in acceptable ways, creating problems for themselves and conflict with others. This provides an opportunity for reimbursement of transformative experiences through NeuroDynamic interventions that will reshape and retrain the brain to become more functional and successful across numerous ecologies.

NeuroDynamic Interventions

NeuroDynamic Interventions (NDIs) are a set of brain-based support strategies used by adults to meet the unmet developmental brain and body needs of a young person. We believe that NeuroDynamic Interventions hold the key to unlocking the requisite knowledge and skills that adults need to assess and work with the young person's behavioral state. They are individually based, relational opportunities that set the stage for transformation. Many of the most challenging interactions that we have with young people occur when there are problems, conflicts, stressful incidents, and inappropriate behavior. Our successful support of young people during these times will frequently come when we are able to either manage or co-manage these challenging behaviors in the moment, particularly when there is the potential of escalation into conflict or crisis. In order to do this successfully, we need to be able to understand how emotions and the brain impact behavior. NDIs use all available momentary information, helping us to take steps towards positively retraining the brain and reshaping the experiences of our young people so that they may be more independent and successful. This momentary management provides temporary therapeutic guidance until other more long-term supports can be put in place. NeuroDynamic knowledge guides adults in determining whether the survival (reactive, non-thinking) or the logical (rational, non-reactive) brain is involved and then assists them in effectively intervening in the moment to stabilize and transform experiences.

How we approach a young person who is exhibiting challenging behavior is critical. Good intentions alone are not enough. NDIs provide the necessary information and skills to create opportunities for new positive experiences that in turn provide opportunities for healthy repair. It is critical that adults fully understand and learn to manage their own responses to the thoughts, feelings, and behaviors of challenging young people. We must keep in mind, that just like young people, when adults are stressed, feeling threatened, or even just overwhelmed, their survival brains can be activated, resulting in unhealthy experiences and interactions. Adults bring with them their own experiences and will benefit from learning to manage them well.

When adults lose their temper or behave irrationally, as you saw in the conflict cycle with Jasper above, the young person learns that such behavior is an acceptable way to deal with conflict, imprinting a volatile experience into the brain for future use. Adults need to be aware of their own emotional triggers, the things that young people do that can make us "see red," and not react without thinking.

Strategy Sheet 7: ACT QUICK

The **ACT QUICK** approach, as presented in The PersonBrain Model, involves a series of NeuroDynamic steps that consider the brain and relational needs of both the young person and the adult. Adults can follow this sequence in order to respond proactively during moments of conflict and crisis. These are your moment-to-moment interactions with young people who require relational support and guidance to prevent escalation or require de-escalation if necessary. If escalation does occur, then the approach provides momentary management until post-conflict/crisis support can be put in place.

ACT QUICK is designed as an efficient tool that can be effective with a variety of issues facing young people. The steps are as follows:

- **A**ssess the brain state of the young person and adult
- **C**alm the young person <u>and</u> environment to ensure safety
- **T**alk with the young person using compassion and natural support
- **Q**uestion for depth and urgency to determine level of support needed
- **U**nwrap meaning of the emotional behavior and thinking
- **I**nvestigate historical experience; is this new or not?
- **C**reate a realistic plan, supported with strengths
- **K**eep in touch; follow up with the young person to show ongoing support

The purpose of the ACT QUICK is to help craft a workable strength plan. The table below gives a brief overview of the essential things that you need to consider for each step.

Step	Questions to Consider
Assess	What is the brain state of the young person: logical (argumentative) or survival (reactive)? What is your brain state? Failure to use your logical brain will result in cognitive combat or an amygdala war, and the conflict could escalate.
Calm	What brain states are in play? Who or what needs to be ecologically managed? What strategies can be implemented for the brain and body to co-regulate or self-regulate?
Talk	Is the young person calm? How can you validate emotional states and connect with the behavior? How intense are their feelings? How can you offer support?
Question	On a scale of 1 to 10, how serious is the problem? What happened? Who was involved? How can you best assist in the resolution of the problem?
Unwrap	Find out the "why" behind the behavior. Was it done consciously or unconsciously? Move on if the answers are filled with "I don't knows."
Investigate	Is the behavior a pattern or a new behavior? Who was involved? What typically has happened if this is a recurring problem?
Create	What strength could a plan/strategy be made around? Practice the strategy considering multiple scenarios. Who else needs to know about this plan?
Keep (in Touch)	Establish a follow-up opportunity. Stay in touch.

Important Note: As with any interaction with young people, issues that reveal the potential for harm to self and others must be reported to the appropriate persons and agencies for enhanced support.

Flexibility in Momentary Management

By this point, it should be clear that consistency is vital to good behavior support. It provides stability and certainty in a world that can often be unstable and unpredictable. It provides a foundation on which to manage expectations and build relationships. But consistency and rigidity are not synonymous when it comes to troubled young people. Yes we need rules, and yes we need to be consistent about how they are applied; but we also need flexibility within our consistency. Being flexible means that you can adapt successfully to changing situations and environments. You can stay calm when facing difficulties; plan ahead, but have options in case things don't work out as anticipated. You can "think on your feet" when circumstances shift and you can persist in the face of unexpected difficulties. Flexibility is a skill that troubled young people desperately need to learn, as rigidity in their responses has not served them well thus far. And just like every other learned skill, flexibility must be modeled.

Remember Ralph and the skateboard from Chapter 4? How that situation was handled is an example of flexibility within consistency. The adult involved kept the big picture in mind, enforcing the rule of not skateboarding in the parking lot, and chose to temporarily ignore the swearing and bad language at that time. She chose to ignore the language in favor of the goal behavior. A more rigid approach would have shifted the focus and sent a completely different message. The adult waited until the next day when Ralph was calm and took him aside for a chat about the language during their encounter the day before. Surprisingly, as soon as she mentioned it, he admitted he was a bit of a "potty mouth" but that he was p*ssed off and it just came out. Because she waited a day, it created a wonderful opportunity to talk about more effective ways of expressing oneself when angry and was another step towards creating new pathways and building their relationship. Rules are rules and expectations should be high, but the flexibility comes in our response to behavior.

Strengths-Based Planning

Until the middle of the 20th century, most psychologists operated in the disease or deficit model. McCashen (2008) explains that from a deficit perspective, once the problem had been identified, all that had to be done was to find an expert who would analyze it and determine the appropriate intervention to fix it. However, this led to simplistic solutions that often did not address the underlying issues and thus returned the focus to the deficit.

Some psychologists believed in a more positive model that focused on optimal functioning. The move away from the "deficit perspective" of psychology to what is now known as "positive psychology" slowly began. The deficit perspective saw problems within the child, with little or no time spent looking at the child's environment. It focused on what had "gone wrong." In contrast, positive psychology focuses on what has "gone right" for the child and in his ecology when assessing, diagnosing, and intervening with young people who are experiencing difficulties. Those who embrace a strengths-based perspective believe that people have strengths, resources, and the ability to recover from adversity. The strengths-based focus uses a different language to describe a person's situation. It focuses on hope and solutions rather than hopelessness and problems. It avoids labels and empowers individuals to become part of the transformational process. McCashen (2008) believes that a strengths-based focus creates positive expectations, that things can be different, and creates opportunities to develop these competencies. A strengths-based planning process does not ignore the problems and difficulties; instead, it identifies the competencies that a person already possesses, what is missing from their life experiences, and the reimbursements that will be used to meet these needs.

The Reimbursements

In Chapter 1, we briefly introduced the six types of NeuroRelational reimbursements: *relational, experiential, biological, regulatory, academic,* and *eco-cultural*. Let's look at each one in detail.

Relational

Relationships are fundamental to therapeutic change. Paul Wachtel (2008) states that human beings exist in relationships. Our brain is a social brain that is constantly redesigning itself to survive. It recognizes when danger is looming or when safety is present. However, when environments change, the brain goes on alert and is extra vigilant to the activity around it. It is critical to remember that the brain has been shaped to survive. It does what experience has shown to be effective based on personal histories. This may mean the brain reacts impulsively or intentionally towards a person or thing within the ecology.

When evidence leads the adult to know that a young person's prior experiences connecting with people have been inadequate or missed completely and are in need of repair or replacement, a relational reimbursement is needed. Poor or non-existent relational attachments create an affective hunger and a desperate need for connection in both emotional and experiential ways. Long, Wood, and Fecser (2001) believe that it is important to implement strategies that influence young people by using the strength of the relationship to convey approval of positive attributes, "thereby strengthening confidence in themselves as valued people." They further state that this type of interaction "promotes qualities like helpfulness, fairness, kindness, leadership, and honesty" (p. 57).

Young people who display oppositional behavior towards others have typically experienced aversive interactions with others who have responded to them with inconsistent, harsh, coercive, and generally ineffective strategies. They often perceive themselves in negative ways and feel that they are "always in trouble" or that someone is always "mad at them." These perceptions breed internal frustration that eventually makes its way to the adult as disturbing behavior. Young people express themselves by modeling the coercive, inconsistent ways of those they have known, and fail to develop adaptive coping skills that resolve internal and external conflicts in constructive ways.

Experiential

From the first moments of life, the brain relies on human experience to learn. We are constantly drawn to interact with others. Experiences teach us what we should or should not do, help us make decisions, and assist us in handling life's situations. They can change how we feel and teach us new things. They shape who we are and who we will become. To really understand something, you need to *experience* it.

Many of the young people we work with have not had the benefit of many of life's positive experiences. Fortunately, experiential reimbursements are often one of the easiest to repair or replace. Experiential reimbursement involves providing needy young people with developmentally necessary opportunities that would typically have been given to children within the same cultural environment.

It is easy for adults to become discouraged when certain social skills are not demonstrated by challenging young people. It is important to remember that experiences are everything in one's life. If a young person has not experienced typical events or had typical positive relationships, he or she will be at a significant disadvantage engaging in daily routines such as eating at restaurants, interacting with other drivers on the road, accepting compliments for good deeds, using the correct silverware during a formal dining experience, etc. In many cases, due to the lack of enriched experience, young people will either avoid these opportunities altogether or approach them with what limited skills they possess. Most try very hard to adapt to and cope with new experiences, but without a fundamental base of social knowledge, they will struggle. True learning can only be gained from actual experience or approximating the experience. That is when you play a significant role.

Neural pathways are developed and modified by life experiences and continue to change throughout life. Pathways that get attention and reinforcement through life experiences are kept and those that do not are eliminated. In addition, the life experiences creating and reinforcing the neural pathways need to be repetitive and occur over a span of time. The brain begins to see patterns in sights, sounds, and movements. The brain begins to build a framework of neural pathways that help us to process the information we are experiencing. The more we experience something, the stronger the pathways will be. As neural pathways are reinforced through experience, they serve as the foundation on which all new information is interpreted, making us capable of negotiating similar but different experiences and making sense of our world.

Biological

For the most part, biological needs are the literal requirements for human survival. If these requirements are not met, the human body simply cannot continue to function. Air, water, and food are metabolic requirements for survival, the most basic need in Maslow's hierarchy. If these needs are not met, they will take precedence over everything else and will dominate behavior. While the needs can be as basic as food, water, or shelter, they can also be pharmacological. Biological reimbursements are not limited to medication. Anything needed to maintain basic body function (like proper nutrition, adequate sleep, a roof over their heads, or proper clothing) will become a priority for disconnected young people. Keep in mind that, according to Maslow's hierarchy of needs, if basic biological needs are not satisfied, then these needs take priority in terms of focus and motivation.

Regulatory

The ability to regulate one's emotional behavior is critical. The amount of personal control we have over what we say, think, or do will determine how well we travel through life. Since emotions are built on genetic and experiential aspects, we should keep these factors in mind when attempting to understand the "why" behind the behaviors our young people demonstrate as signs of their emotional states. We must then begin to teach them more effective ways of regulating themselves when faced with stress or challenge. Without such protective factors, young people will most likely respond in impulsive ways. Impulsivity or reactivity to life will undoubtedly lead to significant coping challenges. As Daniel Siegel (1999) states, the ability to appropriately control our emotions is the "essence of self-regulation" (p. 278).

During the early years of life, caregivers usually undertake the majority of regulation for the child. As we develop, a natural desire to become more independent surfaces. Self-control, or the ability to regulate oneself, will depend on the structure, routine, and experiences that have been historically shared by, and between, the caregivers and the young person. If the caregiver provides sufficient stability, nurturing, and co-regulation, the young person will be better prepared with skills to cope with the natural ups and downs of life. The positive experiences of coping well will inevitably become a part of the mental coping system and ultimately will be imprinted in the memory system as "a tool that worked." When correct tools prove to be beneficial over time and under a variety of circumstances, the tool will be added to the young person's mental toolbox for use in future interactions. This concept becomes important when adults are attempting to understand misbehavior. Linda Lantieri and Daniel Goleman (2008) explain that it is common for adults to mistake "unmanaged stress in our children as (intentional) inappropriate behavior that needs to be stopped." Lantieri and Goleman go on to say that young people are frequently "reprimanded for actions that are really stress reactions, rather than intentional behavior" (p. 12).

Academic

For many challenging young people, school experiences have either been intermittent or extremely negative. They may have academic gaps created by sporadic attendance or have come to see school and teachers as an additional source of stress and possibly threat. Life becomes shaped by reactivations of these memories, and they become the reality of present experience. School and teachers are often not good things in their lives. While negative emotions from threat and stress inhibit learning, arousal and positive emotions contribute significantly to attention, perception, memory, and problem-solving.

Academic reimbursements can take many forms. If a young person is missing key literacy, numeracy, or content skills, programming can be provided to fill those gaps. If negative experiences are the problem, the establishment of positive, non-threatening learning environments can create opportunities for these young people to realize that success at school is a real possibility. In a positive school and classroom climate, all students feel physically safe and emotionally secure. They feel they have a sense of control, have sufficient time to learn, and the ability to deal with or get assistance dealing with their stress. In this climate, they are more likely to be successful and interested in learning. It is important to be mindful of the fact that most disconnected young people in schools are not just disconnected with their academic work but also disconnected with people. Their survival systems are in a state of hyperarousal, ready to strike at any moment and at the least little event.

In far too many instances, educational models fail to address the importance of reconnecting young people with others so that they feel safe and so that they can try new things, take appropriate risks, and pursue challenges more frequently. Increased interpersonal opportunities that result in success will undoubtedly promote greater self-esteem. However, if the student perceives a person called "teacher" or "principal" as negative based on their personal history, relational reimbursement must take place first, or together with the academic reimbursement. People will always be the driving force behind transformation.

Eco-Cultural

Eco-cultural reimbursement is honoring the fact that there are a variety of cultures and sub-cultures, as well as the differences within cultures that exist and need to be tapped into in order for a young person to feel safe and secure. When young people join new environments, their brains are constantly scanning for ways to connect socially in an attempt to survive well. All young people are unique individuals and their experiences, beliefs, values, and language affect their ways of interacting with others. Their brains are a result of their cultural experiences. It is the sights, sounds, tastes, people, ceremonies, and rituals that impact how they filter their world. "Ceremony and ritual give order, stability, and confidence to troubled children and adolescents, whose lives are often in considerable disarray" (Hobbs, 1994, p. 22).

Respect for cultural distinctiveness is important to all young people's sense of self-worth and identity, as well as their sense of belonging. Prior to an adult being able to respond in a culturally empathic and compassionate manner, it is imperative that they interact with each young person as a unique individual according to his or her own particular experiences. The culturally empathic adult understands that the young person's experiences from another culture will always be different from theirs. They must keep in mind how the personal experiences of the young person influence the experiences that they bring to the moment (Stewart, 1989).

Meeting Needs

When you begin to consider a young person's needs, you may find that they require more than one type of reimbursement. In some cases, it is possible that there may be some overlap or gray areas when considering and labeling needs. For example, is a missing cultural experience considered to be an experiential reimbursement or an eco-cultural reimbursement? We would suggest that accuracy about the reimbursement itself is what matters, not the label (although just for the record, we would classify it as eco-cultural because of the culture component). As long as the young person has their needs met, the label becomes less important. Reimbursements involve replacing what is developmentally or relationally owed to the young person in order to provide them with the necessary skills to function effectively in their environment and the flexibility to adjust to unfamiliar environments.

Activity 3: Selecting a Reimbursement to Meet Young People's Needs

Below, you will find 6 short scenarios. Keeping in mind that there may be more than one reimbursement needed, choose the one that you think is the primary reimbursement and briefly explain why you chose that reimbursement as being the one that you would want to begin working with first.

1. Matilda is a 14-year-old who is impulsive and her behavior can be violent and out of control. She lived with her parents until aged 12 when they could no longer manage her behavior at home. She now lives in a residential facility.

Possible Reimbursement: _____

Reason for Choice: _____

_____

_____

2. Nathaniel, age 13, has been known to child protective services for many years due to a series of incidents of physical and sexual abuse perpetrated by his mom's boyfriends. His mom has struggled with chronic depression after growing up in a household of severe abuse and neglect. Nathaniel was referred to child and adolescent mental-health services when he was 11 because of behavior problems at school. He has just been placed in a group home.

Possible Reimbursement: _____

Reason for Choice: _____

_____

_____

3. Jasmine is a bright 10-year-old who lost her biological parents in a car accident at the age of 3. She has had multiple foster placements and been moved many times in the middle of the school year. She has not received a consistent education for several years.

Possible Reimbursement: _____

Reason for Choice: _____

_____

_____

4. Samir, age 16, has a long history of being in care, and an equally long history of mental health issues. When he takes his medication, things go fairly well; however, he often refuses to take his medication, ending up in a perpetual cycle of aggressive behavior towards others and placement breakdown.

Possible Reimbursement: _____

Reason for Choice: _____
_____
_____

5. Rahel is a 10-year-old Syrian girl and the youngest in a family of five other siblings. Her family immigrated to Canada last summer. Soon after arriving, Rahel started having problems with kids at school. They teased her and called her names because of her accent and her clothes, leading to fights and suspension from school. Rahel wanted to be like Canadian kids but her mother felt that she was acting in ways that were unacceptable to their culture and they argued, upsetting both Rahel and her mother.

Possible Reimbursement: _____

Reason for Choice: _____
_____
_____

6. Malik and her younger siblings live with their mother, who works two jobs to make ends meet. She leaves Malik, the oldest, to watch the other children while she works from 4 p.m. to midnight. Malik has had to assume the role of parent and caretaker for her younger siblings and demonstrates "parentified" behaviors towards siblings and peers. Malik tends to be a loner and doesn't have many friends.

Possible Reimbursement: _____

Reason for Choice: _____
_____
_____

Now that you have identified the primary reimbursement, go back to each scenario and decide what other possible types of reimbursements might be considered based on the information provided.

Realistically, most of the young people we work with have complex needs. They come to us with multiple needs that interact with one another. Although there are six types of reimbursements that can be considered, the relational reimbursement will always serve as the foundational reimbursement needed to transform young people successfully. Without quality relationships with people, the brain becomes concerned about survival and will spend a significant amount of time trying to compensate. The personal experiences of the young person will have a direct correlation with how well they can successfully compensate and to what degree reimbursement will be needed.

When considering reimbursements for the young people with whom you work, use the following guiding questions to help determine appropriate reimbursements:

1. What are their existing strengths?
2. What is missing from their life experiences? What do we need to replace?
3. Which particular aspect(s) of reimbursement does the young person need and how might they be repaired? (Repair does not necessarily indicate that a problem must be completely solved. Rather, we feel that repair simply means to bring the young person to a better state that allows for more adaptive functioning and the opportunity to achieve their greatest potential).
4. Who are the key players in the reimbursement process? The goal in each of the reimbursements is to help young people "re-experience" missed opportunities through interactions and/or support. These interactions should always allow for maximum levels of independence and opportunities for input by the young person.

In summary, it is important to ensure that any reimbursement strategy recreates relationships and experiences in order to rewire the brain in more positive, adaptive, and functional ways. It is important to keep in mind that people are the key to this transformation by ensuring the following:

- The young person must have at least one significant adult or quality relationship in their lives that can provide support (Chapter 1 & 2).
- They must feel *safe*, *significant*, *respected*, and *related* (Chapter 3). These are fundamental needs and if they are not met, we know that the brain will focus on these to the exclusion of all else.
- Environments that are *chaotic*, *stressful*, or *traumatic* affect brain development. Young people with these experiences may be overwhelmed and resort to cognitive traps and defense mechanisms (Chapter 4).
- All reimbursement strategies need to be *developmentally appropriate*. They must take into consideration *executive function development* and existential progression (Chapter 5). If there are developmental delays, you need to consider strategies that start where the young person is and go from there. Self-regulatory behavior is not innate. If young people do not self-regulate appropriately, they need to be taught these skills regardless of whether or not they are "old enough to know better"
- Are the adults mismanaging the behavior and *counter-aggressively creating a crisis* (Chapter 6)? Reimbursement strategies can provide skills and replacement behaviors, but these have

to be modeled by the adults because young people learn how to behave by watching and imitating those around them.

Because adults can demonstrate sensitive, caregiving responses to even the most challenging of behaviors by young people, there is a direct correlation with higher levels of positive emotional states, lower levels of negative affect, greater self-esteem, and increased social competence (Suess, Grossman, & Sroufe, 1992). Simply by creating an environment where young people can feel safe, significant, respected, and related, you can begin to set the stage for hopeful transformation and better behavior—positively!

Self-Reflection 16

1) After working through this book, what do you want to change about your practice that will effectively impact the transformation and success of the young people you work with?

_____

_____

_____

_____

_____

_____

2) How can you develop a plan of action to address these changes? Consider staff and administrative support, additional training, and the response of the young people.

_____

_____

_____

_____

_____

_____

3) How will you know if you accomplished your objective? How will you measure and show evidence of change?

_____

_____

_____

_____

_____

_____

References

Ackerman, B. P. & Brown, E. D. (2010). Physical and psychological turmoil in the home and cognitive development. In G. W. Evans & T. D. Wachs (Eds.). *Chaos and its influence on children's development: An ecological perspective.* Washington, DC: American Psychological Association; pp. 35–47.

Ackerman, B. P., Kogos, J., Youngstrom, E., Schoff, K., & Izard, C. (1999). Family instability and the problem behaviors of children from economically disadvantaged families. *Developmental Psychology.* 1999; 35: 258–286.

Addison, J. T. (1992). Urie Bronfenbrenner, *Human Ecology,* 20(2), 16–20.

Ainsworth, M., Blehar, M., Waters, E., & Wall, S. (1978). *Patterns of attachment.* Hillsdale, NJ: Erlbaum.

American Psychiatric Association. (2000). *Diagnostic and statistical manual of mental disorders* (4th ed., rev). Washington, DC: Author.

Amodio, D. M. & Devine, P. G. (2008). On the functions of implicit prejudice and stereotyping: Insights from social neuroscience. In R. E. Petty, R. H. Fazio, & P. Briñol (Eds.). *Attitudes: Insights from the new wave of implicit measures* (pp. 193–226). Hillsdale, NJ: Erlbaum.

Amodio, D. M., Devine, P. G., & Harmon-Jones, E. (2008). Individual differences in the regulation of intergroup bias: The role of conflict monitoring and neural signals for control. *Journal of Personality and Social Psychology, 94,* 60–74.

Andreasen, N. C. (2005). *The creating brain: The neuroscience of genius.* Washington, DC: Danna Press.

Anglin, J. P. (2003). *Pain, normality and the struggle for congruence: Reinterpreting residential care for children and youth.* Haworth: Binghamton, New York.

Anglin, J. P. (2013). Working in the children's best interests: Differences that make a difference. *Child and Youth Care Work.* 31(1): 4–10.

Badenoch, B. (2008). *Being a brain-wise therapist: A practical guide to interpersonal neurobiology.* New York: Norton.

Baker, P. & White-McMahon, M. (2014). *The hopeful brain: Neurorelational repair for disconnected children and youth.* Raleigh, NC: Lulu.

Barton, S., Gonzalez, R., & Tomlinson, P. (2012). *Therapeutic residential care for children and young people: An attachment and trauma-informed model for practice.* Philadelphia, PA: Jessica Kingsley.

Baumeister, R. F., & Leary, M. R. (1995). The need to belong. Desire for interpersonal attachments as a fundamental human motivation. *Psychological Bulletin, 117,* 497-529.

Bell, M. A. & Calkins, S. D. (2012). *Attentional control and emotion regulation in early development.* In M. Posner (Ed.), Cognitive neuroscience of attention. 2nd Guilford Press; New York, NY.

Bertenthal, B. I., Greenback, G., & Boyer, T. W. (2013). Differential contributions of development and learning to infants' knowledge of object continuity and discontinuity. *Child Development,* 84(2): 413–421.

Blakemore, S-J. & Choudhury, S. (2006). Development of the adolescent brain: implications for executive function and social cognition. *Journal of Child Psychology and Psychiatry,* 47: 296–312. doi: 10.1111/j.1469-7610.2006.01611.x

Bloom, S. L. (2013). *Creating sanctuary: Toward the evolution of sane societies.* New York, NY: Routledge.

Bloom, S. L. (2005). The sanctuary model of organizational change for children's residential treatment. *Therapeutic community: The international journal for therapeutic and supportive organizations.* 26(1): 65–81.

Bloom, S. L. (1997). *Creating sanctuary: Toward the evolution of sane societies.* (1997). New York: Routledge.

Bobula, K. A. (2011). *This is your brain on bias … or, the neuroscience of bias.* Retrieved from: http://www.twotowns.org/wp/wp-content/uploads/2014/05/This-is-your-brain-on-bias%E2%80%A6-or-the-neuroscience-of-bias.pdf

Borba, M. (2012, October 3). *Dr. Borba on teaching respect* [Web log post]. Retrieved from http://www.itwixie.com/uncategorized/dr-borba-on-teaching-respect

Bowlby, J. (1969). *Attachment and loss, vol. 1: Attachment.* New York: Basic Books.

Bronfenbrenner, U. (1979). *The ecology of human development.* Cambridge, MA: Harvard University Press.

Brofenbrenner, U. & Evans, G. W. (2000). Developmental science in the 21st century: Emerging theoretical models, research designs, and empirical findings. *Social Development, 9,* 115–125.

Carter, C. S. (1998). Neuroendocrine perspectives on social attachment and love. *Psychoneuroendocrinology, 23,* 779–818.

Casey, B. J., & Jones, R. M. (2010). "Neurobiology of the Adolescent Brain and Behavior." *Journal of the American Academy of Child and Adolescent Psychiatry,* 49(12): 1189–1285.

Centre for Addiction and Mental Health. (2013, January 15). Youth mentoring linked to many positive effects, new study shows. *ScienceDaily.* Retrieved February 29, 2016 from www.sciencedaily.com/releases/2013/01/130115143850.htm

Cohen, J. A., Berliner, L., & Mannarino, A. (2010). *Trauma focused CBT for children with co-occuring trauma and behavior problems.* doi: 10.1016/j.chiabu.2009.12.003

Coldwell, J., Pike, A., & Dunn, J. (2006). Household chaos – links with parenting and child behavior. *Journal of Child Psychology and Psychiatry,* 47(11): 1116–1122.

Cole, S. O., O'Brien, J. G., Gadd, M. G., Ristuccia, J. M., Wallace, D. L., & Gregory, M. (2005). *Helping traumatized children learn: Supportive school environments for children traumatized by family violence.* Boston, MA.: Massachusetts Advocates for Children.

Conflict. (n.d.). In Merriam-Webster's online dictionary. Retrieved March 5, 2016 from http://www.merriam-webster.com/dictionary/conflict

Conklin, H. M., Luciana, M., Hooper, C., & Yarger, R. S. (2007). Working memory performance in typically developing children and adolescents: Behavioral evidence of protracted frontal lobe development. *Journal of Child Psychology and Psychiatry,* 31(1): 103–128.

Coopersmith, S. (1967). *The antecedents of self-esteem.* San Francisco, CA: W. H. Freeman.

Crisis. (n.d.). In Merriam-Webster's online dictionary. Retrieved March 5, 2016 from http://www.merriam-webster.com/dictionary/crisis

Cozolino, L. (2006). *The neuroscience of human relationships.* New York: WW Norton & Co., Inc.

Damasio, A. (1994). *Descartes' error: Emotion, reason, and the human brain.* New York: Norton.

Dawson, E., Shear, P. K., & Stratkowski, S. M. (2012). Behavior regulation and mood predict social functioning among healthy young adults. *Journal of Clinical and Experimental Neuropsychology,* 34(3): 297–305.

Decety, J. (2010). The neuroscience of empathy in humans. *Developmental Neuroscience*. doi: 10.1159/000317771

Devinsky, O. (2000). Right cerebral hemisphere dominance for a sense of corporeal and emotional self. *Epilepsy and Behavior, 1,* 60–73.

Diamond, A. (1990a). Developmental time course in human infants and infant monkeys, and the neural bases of inhibitory control in reaching. *Annals of the New York Academy of Sciences,* 608: 637–676.

Diamond, A. (1990b). The development of neural bases and memory functions as indexed by the AB and delayed response tasks in human infants and human monkeys. *Annals of the New York Academy of Sciences,* 608: 267–317.

Doidge, N. (2007). *The brain that changes itself.* New York: Penguin Books.

Dunn, J. & Plomin, R. (1990). *Separate lives: Why siblings are so different.* New York, NY: Basic Books.

Elizinga, B. & Roelofs, K. (2005). Cortisol-induced impairments of working memory requires acute sympathetic activation. *Behavioral Neuroscience, 119,* 98–103.

Erikson, Erik H. (1993, reissue). *Childhood and Society.* New York: W. W. Norton & Company.

Evans, G. W. (2006). Child development and the physical environment. *Annual Review of Psychology,* 57: 423–451.

Evans, G. W., Gonnella, C., Marcynyszyn, L. G., & Salpekar, N. (2005). The role of chaos in poverty and children's socioemotional adjustment. *Psychological Science,* 16(7): 560–565.

Evans, G. W. & Wachs, T. D. (2010). Chaos in context. In G. W. Evans & T. D Wachs (Eds.). *Chaos and its influence on children's development: An ecological perspective.* Washington, DC.: APA.

Figley, C. R. (1995). *Compassion fatigue: Coping with secondary traumatic stress disorder in those who treat the traumatized.* New York: Brunner/Mazel, Inc.

Friedman, N. P., Miyake, A., Corley, R. P., Young, S. E., DeFries, J. C., & Hewitt, J. K. (2006). Not all executive functions are related to intelligence. *Psychological Science,* 17, 173–179.

Garfat, T. (2008). The inter-personal in-between: An exploration of relational child and youth care practice. In G. Bellefeuille & F. Ricks (Eds.), *Standing on the precipice: Inquiry into the creative potential of child and youth care practice.* Edmonton. AB: MacEwan Press.

Garon, N., Bryson, S. E., & Smith, I. M. (2008). Executive functioning preschoolers: A review using an integrative framework. *Psychological Bulletin,* 134: 31–60.

Goleman, D. (2006). *Social intelligence.* New York: Bantam Dell.

Goleman, D. (1998). *Working with emotional intelligence.* New York: Bantam Books.

Hart S. A., Petrill S. A., Deater Deckard, K., Thompson L. A. (2007). SES and CHAOS as environmental mediators of cognitive ability: A longitudinal genetic analysis. *Intelligence,* 35(3): 233–242.

Hawkley, L. C., Masi, C. M., Berry, J. D., & Cacioppo, J. T. (2006). Loneliness is a unique predictor of age-related differences in systolic blood pressure. *Psychological Aging,* 21(1): 152–164.

Hebb, D. O. (1949). *The organization of behavior.* New York: Wiley & Sons.

Hobbs, N. (1994). *The troubled and troubling child.* Cleveland, OH: American Re-Education Association.

International Institute for Restorative Practices (2009). *Improving school climate: Findings from schools implementing restorative practice*s. International Institute for Restorative Practices. Bethlehem, PA.

Isquith, P. K., Gioia, G. A., & Espy, K. A. (2004). Executive function in preschool children: Examination through everyday behavior. *Developmental Neuropsychology,* 26: 403–422.

Jacobs Bao, K. & Lyubomirsky, S. (2003). Making happiness last. In A. Parks (Ed.), *The handbook of positive interventions.* New York, NY: Wiley-Interscience.

Jones, S. M. (2011). Supportive Listening. *International Journal of Listening.* doi: 10.1080/10904018.2011.536475

Kaplow, J. B. & Widom, C. S. (2007). Age of onset of child maltreatment predicts long-term mental health outcomes. *Journal of Abnormal Psychology,* 116(1), 176–187.

Kirkorian, H. L, Pempek, T. A., Murphy, L. A., Schmidt, M. E., & Anderson, D. R. (2009). The impact of background television on parent-child interaction. *Child Development,* 80(3): 1350–1359.

Landhuis C. E, Poulton, R., Welch, D., & Hancox R. J. (2007). Does childhood television viewing lead to attention problems in adolescence? Results from a prospective longitudinal study. *Pediatrics,* 120(3): 532–537.

Lantieri, L. & Goleman, D. (2008). *Building emotional intelligence: Techniques to cultivate inner strength in children.* Boulder, CO: Sounds True.

Lawrence-Lightfoot, S. (2000). *Respect: An exploration.* Cambridge, Mass.: Perseus.

LeDoux, J. E. (1996). *The emotional brain.* New York: Simon and Schuster.

LeSure-Lester, G. E. (2000). Relationship between empathy and aggression and behavior compliance among abused group home youth. *Child Psychiatry and Human Development,* 31(3): 153–161.

Long, N. J. (1995). Why adults strike back: Learned behavior or genetic code? *Reclaiming Children and Youth: Journal of Emotional and Behavioral Problems,* 3(1): 11–15.

Long, N. J. (2007). The conflict cycle paradigm: How troubled students get teachers out of control. In N. J. Long, F. A. Fecser, W. C. Morse, & R. G. Newman (Eds.). *Conflict in the classroom: Positive staff support for troubled students* (6th ed.). Austin, TX. Pro-Ed.

Long, N. J. (2014). The conflict cycle paradigm: How troubled students get teachers out of control. In N. J. Long, F. A. Fecser, W. C. Morse, R. G. Newman, & J. E. Long (Eds.). *Conflict in the classroom: Successful behavior management using the psychoeducational model* (7th ed.). Austin, TX. Pro-Ed.

Long, N. J. (1965). *Direct help to the classroom teacher.* Washington, DC: School Research Project, Washington School of Psychiatry.

Long, N. J., Wood, M., & Fecser, F. A. (2001). *Advanced instruction in life space crisis intervention: The skill of reclaiming young people involved in self-defeating patterns of behavior.* Hagerstown, MD: Life Space Crisis Intervention Institute.

Maier, H. (1987). Children and youth develop and grow in youth care. *Child and Youth Services,* 9(2): 9–33.

Manly, J. T., Kim, J. E., Rogosch, F. A., & Cicchetti, D. (2001). Dimensions of child maltreatment and children's adjustment: Contributions of developmental timing and subtype. *Development and Psychopathology,* 3(4), 759–782.

Martin, A., Razza, R., & Brooks-Gunn, J. (2012). Specifying the links between household chaos and preschool children's development. *Early Child Development and Care,* 182(10), 1247–63.

Matheny, A. P., Jr., Wachs, T. D., Ludwig, J. L., & Phillips, K. (1995). Bringing order out of chaos: Psychometric characteristics of the Confusion, Hubbub, and Order Scale. *Journal of Applied Developmental Psychology.* 16: 429–444.

Maslow, Abraham (1954). *Motivation and personality.* New York: Harper.

Maxwell, L. E. & Evans G. W. (2000). The effects of noise on pre-school children's pre-reading skills. *Journal of Environmental Psychology,* 20: 91–97.

McCashen, W. (2008). *The strengths model.* Victoria: St. Luke's Innovative Resources.

McDonald, N. M., & Messinger, D. S. (2014). *The development of empathy: How, when, and why.* Retrieved April 25, 2016 from https://www.researchgate.net/profile/Nicole_Mcdonald/publications

Miyake, A, Friedman, N. P., Emerson, M. J., Witzki, A. H., Howerter, A., & Wager, T. D. (2000). The unity and diversity of executive functions and their contributions to complex "frontal lobe" tasks: a latent variable analysis. *Cognitive Psychology,* 41: 49–100. doi:10.1006/cogp.1999.0734

Miller, G. E., Chen, E. & Fok, A. K. (2009). Low early-life social class leaves a biological residue manifested by decreased glucocorticoid and increased pro inflammatory signalling. *Proceedings of the National Academy of Sciences USA,* 106, 14716–14721.

Miller, G. E., Chen, E., & Zjou, E. S. (2007). If it goes up, must it come down? Chronic stress and the hypothalamic-pituitary-adrenocortical axis in humans. *Psychological Bulletin,* 133, 24–45.

Miner, J. L. & Clarke-Stewart, K. A. (2008). Trajectories of externalizing behavior from age 2 to age 9: Relations with gender, temperament, ethnicity, parenting, and rater. *Developmental Psychology,* 44(3): 771–786.

Morrow, K. V. & Styles, M. B. (1995). *Building relationships with youth in program settings: A study of Big Brothers/Big Sisters programs.* Retrieved April 25, 2016 from http://www.issuelab.org/resource/building_relationships_with_youth_in_program_settings_a_study_of_big_brothersbig_sisters

Nadler, A., Malloy, T. E., & Fisher, J. D. (2008). Intergroup reconciliation: Dimensions and themes. In A. Nadler, T. E. Malloy, & J. D. Fisher (Eds.). *The social psychology of intergroup reconciliation.* New York, NY: Oxford University Press.

Pavey, L., Greitemeyer, T., & Sparks, P. (2011). Highlighting relatedness promotes prosocial motives and behavior. *Personality and Social Psychology Bulletin,* 37(7): 905–917.

Pettinelli. M. (2015). *How does cognition influence emotion?* Raleigh, NC: Lulu.

Perry, B. (2014). *Helping traumatized children: A brief overview for caregivers.* Retrieved February 28, 2016 from https://childtrauma.org/wp-content/uploads/2014/01/Helping_Traumatized_Children_Caregivers_Perry1.pdf

Perry, B., Pollard, R. A., Blakely, T. L., Baker, W. L., & Vigilante, D. (1995). Childhood trauma, the neurobiology of adaptation, and "use-dependent" development of the brain: How "states" become "traits." *Infant Mental Health Journal,* 16(4), 271–291.

Porges, S. W. (2011). *The polyvagal theory: Neurophysiological foundations of emotions, attachment, communication, self-regulation.* New York, NY: Norton.

Powell, K. (2006). "How does the teenage brain work?" *Nature,* August 2006.

Pryce, J. (2012). Mentor attunement: An approach to successful school-based mentoring relationships. *Child and Adolescent Social Work Journal.* doi: 10.1007/s10560-012-0260-6

Putnam, F. (1997). *Dissociation in children and adolescents: A developmental perspective.* New York: Guildford Press.

Putnam, F. W., Helmers, K., & Trickett, P. K. (1993). Development, reliability and validity of a child dissociation scale. *Child Abuse and Neglect,* 17: 731–741.

Pynoos, R. S. & Nader, K. (1988). Psychological first aid and treatment model to children exposed to community violence. *Journal of Traumatic Stress,* 1: 445–473.

Pynoos, R. S., Steinberg, A. M., Ornitz, E. M., & Neneroff, C. B. (1997). Issues in the developmental neurobiology of traumatic stress. In R. Yehudi & A. McFarlane (Eds.). *Psychobiology of post traumatic stress disorder,* pp. 176-194. New York: New York Academy of Sciences.

Ratey, J, (2001). *The user's guide to the brain.* New York: Random House.

Restack, R. (2006). *The naked brain: How the emerging neurosociety is changing how we live, work and love.* New York, NY: Harmony.

Riestenberg, N. (2002). *Restorative measures in schools: Evaluation results.* Paper presented at the Third International Conference on Conferencing, Circles and other Restorative Practices, Minneapolis, MN, USA.

Sapolsky, R. M. (2004). *Why zebras don't get ulcers.* New York: Henry Holt and Company.

Sapolsky, R. M., Romero, L. M., & Munck, A. U. (2000). How do glucocorticoids influence stress responses? Integrating permissive, suppressive, stimulatory, and preparative actions. *Endocrine Review,* 21, 55–89.

Schore, A. N. (1994). *Affect regulation and the origin of the self: The neurobiology of emotional development.* Hillsdale, NJ: Erlbaum.

Seligman, M (1995). *The optimistic child: Proven program to safeguard children from depression & build lifelong resilience*. New York: Houghton Mifflin.

Shepard, L. (2015, April 28). Personal Interview.

Siegel, D. (2007). *The mindful brain: Reflection and attunement in the cultivation of well-being*. New York, NY: Norton.

Siegel, D. (1999). *The developing mind: How relationships and the brain interact to shape who we are*. New York, NY: The Guilford Press.

Sousa, D. A. (2007). *How the special needs brain learns* (2nd ed.). Thousand Oaks, CA: Corwin Press.

Sousa, D. A. (2009). *How the brain influences behavior: Management strategies for every classroom*. Thousand Oaks, CA: Corwin Press.

Springer, M. V., McIntosh, A. R., Wincour, C., & Grady, C. L. (2005). The relation between brain activity during memory tasks and years of education in young and older adults. *Neuropsychology, 19*(2), 181–192.

Stewart, I. (1989). *Transactional analysis counselling in action*. London: Sage.

Stien, P. T. & Kendall, J. (2004). *Psychological trauma and the developing brain: Neurologically based interventions for challenging children*. New York: Routledge.

Suess, G. J., Grossman, K. E., & Sroufe, L. A. (1992). Effects of attachment to mother and father on quality of adaptation: From dyadic to individual organization of self. *International Journal of Behavioral Development, 15*, 43–65.

Terr, L. (1981). Forbidden games. *Journal of the American Academy of Child Psychiatry,* 20: 741–760.

Terr, L. (1990). *Too scared to cry*. New York: Basic Books.

Townsend, B. L. (2000). The disproportionate discipline of African-American learners: Reducing school suspensions and expulsions. *Exceptional Children, 66*, 381–391.

Valentine, M. (1994). *How to deal with difficult discipline problems in the school*. Dubuque. IA. Kendall/Hunt.

Valiente, C., Lemery-Chalfant, K., & Reiser, M. (2007). Pathways to problem behaviors: Chaotic homes, parent and child effortful control, and parenting. *Social Development,* 16: 249–267.

Van der Kolk, B. (1996). The body keeps score: Memory and the evolving psychobiology of posttraumatic stress. *Harvard Review of Psychiatry, 1,* 253–265.

Wachtel, P. L. (2008). *Relational theory and the practice of psychotherapy.* New York, NY: Guilford Press.

Wood, M. M., Quirk, C. A., & Swindle, F. L. (2007). *Reaching responsible behavior: Development therapy-developmental teaching for troubled children and adolescents* (4th ed.). Austin, TX: ProEd.

Zelazo, P. D., Muller, U., Frye, D., & Marcovitch, S. (2003). The development of executive function in early childhood. *Monographs of the Society for Research in Child Development, 68:* 3 (Serial No. 274).

Zelechoski, A. D., Sharma, R., Beserra, K., Miguel, J. L., DeMarco, M., & Spinazzola, J. (2013). Traumatized youth in residential treatment settings: Prevalence, clinical presentation, treatment, and policy implications. *Journal of Family Violence.* doi: 10.1007/s10896-013-9534-9